LIFE HERE AND HEREAFTER

LIFE HERE AND HEREAFTER

Automatic writing received mostly through the pencil of Charlotte E.Dresser ("Sis")

Edited by

Fred Rafferty ("F. R.")

A sequel to *Spirit World and Spirit Life*

WHITE CROW

www.whitecrowbooks.com

Life Here and Hereafter

Original copyright © 1927 by Fred Raffrerty, Santa Ana, California.
This copyright © 2025 by White Crow Productions Ltd. All rights reserved.
Published by White Crow Books, an imprint of White Crow Productions Ltd.

The right of the author has been asserted in accordance with
the Copyright, Design and Patents act 1988.

A CIP catalogue record for this book is available from the British Library.
For information, contact White Crow Books by e-mail: info@whitecrowbooks.com.

Cover Design by Astrid@Astridpaints.com
Interior design by Velin@Perseus-Design.com

Paperback: ISBN: 9781786772947
eBook: ISBN: 9781786772954

Non-Fiction / BODY, MIND & SPIRIT / Afterlife & Reincarnation

www.whitecrowbooks.com

PREFACE

~

In a former volume, *Spirit World and Spirit Life*, the conditions and activities which prevail in the future life are quite clearly portrayed by selections from our records received through automatic writing. In giving to the world a second volume based on these records,—which have been received mostly through Miss Dresser's pencil,—we have in Part II emphasized a phase of that life that most books of this nature have mentioned but little. It seems so vital to our friends on the other side, and they have made it seem so vital to us, that we feel it a duty to present it fully. Some may question our judgment in giving space for so many of the accounts; but we want to try to make the world understand that it is a very real condition. Time and time again it is impressed upon us that most people here are, through ignorance, and sometimes through willful ignorance, placing obstacles in the path of their progress which will cause them much trouble and delay when entering upon their spirit life. It is with the hope that these accounts will remove a little of that ignorance, and aid in understanding the life on the other side of the veil, that they are given to the public. They are not fiction by any means, as the reader will soon ascertain if he uses his brain to try to comprehend what they really mean.

The other sections of the book are given over to further selections from our records on various subjects, some of which are more fully treated in the previous book. It is hoped that this volume will meet with as friendly a reception as did its predecessor.

As stated in the introductory chapter, the editor of these writings did not acquire the ability to receive messages until some two years ago. A number of the various articles that have come through his pencil are included, and it may be advisable to designate them by the following page numbers:—

7	73	115 to 118	163
16	76	122	177
21-30	82	126	199
31	83	138	229
35	84	142	233
57	91	143	238
58	94	144	240
68 partly 96	103	150 a portion	
70			

All the others, with the possible exception of one or two paragraphs, came through Miss Dresser's pencil, as stated above.

Fred Rafferty, Charlotte E. Dresser,
Santa Ana, California.
October 19, 1926.

CONTENTS

~

PREFACE V

INTRODUCTORY 1

PART I: LIFE IN THE SPIRIT WORLD.................................. **5**

    BELIEF IN SPIRIT LIFE   6

    FIRST EXPERIENCES   7

    THE STUDENT   11

    THE PARTNERS   16

    EARTHQUAKE VICTIMS   18

    A SPIRIT FROM EARLIEST TIMES   19

    A SPIRIT FROM THE TIME OF CROMWELL   21

    THE SMALL MERCHANT   23

    A WOMAN's EXPERIENCE   25

    THE NEWCOMER   26

    THE STORY OF THE SCHOOL TEACHER   28

    DIFFERENT VIEWPOINTS   30

    THE ORDINARY BUSINESSMAN   31

    SEEKING EARTH FRIENDS   33

    MYSTICISM   35

    A CASE OF OBSESSION   36

    VARIOUS MESSAGES   43

    THE CHINESE PHILOSOPHER AND RELIGION   57

    THINKING   58

GHOSTS	61
INFANTS IN SPIRIT LAND	63
MISCELLANEOUS ADVICE	68
RIGHT LIVING	70
THE EARTH ONLY A SCHOOL	71
PERSONALITY	72
SPIRIT INFLUENCE ON EARTH LIFE	73
THE LIFE ON EARTH	75
MAKING US UNDERSTAND	76
THE REALITY OF SPIRIT LAND	76
TWO VISITORS	77
THE BAND OF WORKERS	78
WORKING THROUGH DIVINE INFLUENCE	79
THE MINISTER	80
EVIDENTIAL MESSAGES	82
THE DESIRE TO HELP	83
JOAN OF ARC	83
SIGHT	84
THE WATCHERS	85
THE VALUE OF COMMUNICATION	85
DEATH	86
THE JOY OF SPIRIT LIFE	87
THE SPIRIT BODY AND SPIRIT CONDITIONS	88
LIFE	90
THE HUMORIST	91
AN EXPERIENCE	92
A DAY IN SPIRIT LAND	93
DEE	94
TIME	95
PHILOSOPHY	96
THE INTERFERING SPIRITS	97
PRIVACY OF THOUGHT RESPECTED	98
THE NEIGHBOR SPIRITS	99
OBSESSION	99
THE SCANDINAVIAN	100
THE SOUL	101
AN ACQUAINTANCE	102

CONTENTS

FROM A NOTED PSYCHOLOGIST	103
SOME STRANGERS	104
A SCHOOL FRIEND	105
SPIRIT PLANES AND RACE PROBLEMS	106
COMMENTS	107
SPIRIT SENSES AND EARTH VIBRATIONS	108
STAY BY THE TRUTH	108
THE "SUNSHINE" FRIENDS	108
THE ALL-WISE POWER	111
PRAYER	111
DIFFICULTIES OF COMMUNICATION	112
THE JOKERS	112
AN OLD FRIEND	113
THE UNKNOWN COMMUNICATORS	114
LIFE AND CHARACTER	115
THE CARE OF LITTLE CHILDREN	115
BELIEVERS IN MYSTICISM	117
EVIL SPIRITS	118
A SUNDAY SERMON	119
HELPING OTHERS	120
HEAVEN IS WIDE	121
UNDERSTANDING LIFE	122
UNCONSCIOUSNESS AFTER DEATH	122
EVIDENTIAL TESTS AND PROPHECIES	123
RELIGIOUS SERVICE	124
A CONCEPTION OF GOD	125
DESIRE FOR RECOGNITION	126
FORGETTING	127
SELFISHNESS AND SIN	127
THE COMMUNICATING CIRCLE	128
LAST CENTURY EXPERIMENTS	129
DEATH FROM ACCIDENT	130
OUR FIRST EXPERIENCES	131
THEIR "USUAL" LIVES	131
WHAT WE CAN DO	132
SPIRIT SIGHT	133
MARY's MESSAGE	134

GUIDES   135
THE UNBELIEVER   136
SWEDENBORG   137
FROM THE CHINESE PHILOSOPHER   138
IMPERFECT COMMUNICATION   138
MESSENGERS   139
THINKING SPIRITUALLY   139
SPIRIT CLOTHES   140
THE SPIRIT HOME   142
THE SCIENTIFIC CIRCLE   142
SPIRIT COMMUNICATION   143
THE GREAT ADVENTURE   144
GLEANINGS   144

PART II: UNDEVELOPED SPIRITS.....................**149**
UNDEVELOPED SPIRITS   150
STORIES OF UNDEVELOPED SPIRITS   162
FURTHER ACCOUNTS OF UNDEVELOPED SPIRITS   184
THE BUSINESSMAN   185
THE SHOP GIRL   189
THE SPORTSMAN   191
THE FOOTBALL PLAYER   194
THE FARMER   199
ANOTHER BUSINESSMAN   202
THE TRAVELING MAN   205
THE MILLWORKER   207
THE BOY   210
THE WASHWOMAN   212
THE GIRL   214
THE LONELY NEWCOMER   216
THE WANDERER   218
THE CHILD   221
THE VICTIM OF BAD LIQUOR   222
THE SUICIDE   225
THE WOMAN FROM INDIA   227
THE PRISONER   229
THE DISSATISFIED MAN   231

CONTENTS

THE CRIMINAL   233
A SPIRIT WHO IS OBSESSED   235
WRONGLY EXECUTED   238
THE PEASANT WOMAN   240
A TERRIBLE ACCIDENT   242
THE AUTOMOBILE ACCIDENT   244
ANOTHER AUTOMOBILE VICTIM   246
THE CAMP-MEETING CONVERT   248

APPENDIX..**253**

MENTAL PROCESSES   253
THE SUBCONSCIOUS MIND   261
STUDY AND EDUCATION   267
COMMUNICATION BETWEEN SPIRITS   268
EVOLUTION   270
THE CHINESE PHILOSOPHER   271
THE GEOGRAPHY OF THE HEAVENLY SPHERES   276

INTRODUCTORY

~

Communications from the spirit world come in numerous ways. The most voluminous records are probably those made by automatic writing, where the medium, sometimes entranced, but more often not, writes ideas and statements that are seemingly more or less foreign to the conscious thought. This method undoubtedly lends itself readily to the operation of the medium's subconscious mind; and, unquestionably, much that there purports to be from spirit sources originates in, or at least is greatly modified by, this little known portion of the mentality. But there are often evidences in the manner or the content of the writing that, to a truly unprejudiced mind, indicate a source entirely outside the medium. The editor believes that the material included in this book belongs in this class, although it is hardly possible here to enter into much detailed explanation regarding the proof of it. It is hoped that the reader is familiar with a previous volume called *Spirit World and Spirit Life* where some of the proof is set forth and he is also referred to the article on the subconscious mind in the appendix of this book. To aid those who have not had the opportunity to read the first volume, some facts should be presented here that will make clear the origin of both books.

For many years three of us were in very close friendship and companionship. We were together much of the time, and traveled extensively over a good portion of the globe. The constant association led to the adoption among ourselves of the intimate appellations of "Dee," "Sis," and "F. R." Late in 1917 our joys were rudely interrupted by the death of my wife, "Dee." "Sis" had always looked forward to, or at least hoped for, a future life. I had seldom given the subject a thought. But in less than a year, through "table-tipping" at the home of some friends, and later through the Ouija board by ourselves, we were drawn into communication with unseen forces that soon proved themselves to be "Dee" and the friends she had already made in the spirit world. Communications came rapidly. Information was given freely. And we were soon made acquainted with the life and conditions in that farther existence. The leader of the communicating circle on that side gave us her name as "Mary." And "Mary" and "Dee" have now for over eight years been in almost daily touch with us. Sis soon developed automatic writing under their guidance; and, after repeated trials extending over more than six years, my hand received the gift also, but in a rather unusual manner. For despite the hundreds of trials, I cannot receive an impression unless Sis's hand is placed on mine. The writing is usually a little freer if she places it on the hand that holds the pencil; but much of my writing has come when her hand is placed on my left hand, which is quiet.

In 1922 we published a portion of the writings that came through Sis's pencil under the title, *Spirit World and Spirit Life*. This book has just been reissued in a slightly revised and enlarged form, and an acquaintance with its contents will aid somewhat in estimating the value of the statements made in this volume.

The first volume deals with Communication; Evidential Messages; The Spirit Body; Spirit Life; Progress; Music; Art and Beauty, etc., an engaging description of the life and happiness of the spirit who is advancing joyously towards life's goal. But as our education advanced also, we were made aware that not all spirits enter at once into these conditions. We learn that very, very many are more or less delayed for various reasons, and that some encounter, obstacles which hinder their progress for long periods. It is to this class that Part II of this volume is devoted; and we trust the reader will study it carefully and thoughtfully. It is a subject that has been brought to the attention of very few people, but is one that concerns each and all of us, if we wish to avoid the effects of selfishness and materialistic thought, and participate without unnecessary trouble and delay in the glories of the heavenly existence.

PART I

LIFE IN THE SPIRIT WORLD

BELIEF IN SPIRIT LIFE

"We know your great desire to learn the truth, and we are allowed to answer that desire, for we are the truth, the truth of life eternal. We are the proof of the farther life to which all must come, and we are here to give unmistakable evidence of the life eternal. We too were mortals, we too suffered the earth life with all its mistaken beliefs, its poverty of thought and ideals. But even so, we are here to bear testimony to the final uplift of the soul, and its indescribable power of growth and progress. Believe in us. Believe in a just and true God who adds to our poor earthborn lives, with their darkened beliefs and groping knowledge, the pure heavenly existence with its first real liberty of choice and progress."

'Why do you say the first real liberty?'

"Because we began our earthly existence with tendencies and characteristics for which we were not responsible, and which fettered our liberty."

'But do you not begin that life still fettered by earthborn habits?'

"Yes, partially. But think how many chains have been removed: physical weakness, the fight against poverty, the necessary effort to gain a living, race problems, and many others. We are at least free from these."

"It is a sorrowful condition we behold on earth, and we wish to try to give a new thought that will turn the world to better things. It is not easy to say something really new; you have exhortations from the pulpits that should be sufficient. But they seem to have lost their effect. We know that materialism is leading many into habits of life and thought that will defer their awakening and advance here very seriously. This is not necessary for most of them, for they are not evil, and in many cases not especially selfish. But the strong thought that they hold, that *there is no future life*, reacts upon them to such an extent that they fail to respond to the influences here after they arrive. We have no influence upon such people while they are on earth, of course. If we did, they would not be adopting these wrong beliefs."

FIRST EXPERIENCES

"I am not a novice in this life anymore. I have been on this side for fifteen years, and have been in active service most of the time. But I was a beginner at one time, as all are who come here. No one arrives with full-fledged spirit powers. It is easy for some to begin to use their spirit sight and hearing, but it was difficult for me. I had not given a thought in earth life to what would be necessary in this. I did believe in a future life, and I was not long in a really unconscious state after arriving. But I was grievously disappointed at first that I did not find the beautiful heavenly life which I had been taught to expect.

"It was not entire darkness; I could see dimly. But all that was visible was drab and unattractive. I could hear nothing, and could see no living being. You can imagine a little how surprised I was and how puzzled. I knew that my earth life was over; I had been very ill, and had been conscious until nearly the last. So there was no misunderstanding about the fact that I had died. But I could not understand what existence could mean, where there was so little I could see, and nothing I could hear.

"After a time—I don't know how long it was—I realized that there were other beings near me. I was conscious at times of shadow-like forms that moved. I watched them, trying to understand what they meant. I was not particularly interested, for I did not in the least suspect that they were beings like myself. If I thought anything, it was that they were animals of some kind.

"I was, of course, not in full possession of my reasoning faculties. When spirit first throws off the material envelope, there is a shock—not always a severe one, but often sufficient to leave the mentality in a dazed condition, hardly more than a dream-like state. If I had then possessed full powers of reasoning, I could no doubt have soon concluded that the shadows meant something to me. But at first I simply watched them curiously. They came and went, sometimes a few, sometimes many. I think it must have been months before it dawned upon me that they might be spirits. Then I began to really think things out. I first concluded that possibly spirit was always rather ghostly; possibly these shadows were only conscious of me as a shadow. I pondered over this for some time. I finally concluded that there must be more to heaven than such shadowy creations. Something must be wrong somewhere. I made no attempt to study myself, I only wondered about the others. Why were they unable to make a more solid appearance?

"It was a long study; and only after extended cogitation did I suddenly begin to wonder if the fault might lie with me. This thought interested me tremendously. I began to speculate on what spirit sight might be like, and I soon saw that it would necessarily be different from earthly sight. I was not successful in my conclusions at first as to the method by which I would have to see, but I was able to perceive things more plainly just because I realized that I myself was the one at fault. When we realize our own shortcomings, a great advance is made toward eliminating them, no matter what they are.

"I was soon conscious that I had greatly increased my powers of vision, for I could now see these other beings quite plainly. And I saw that they were conscious of my presence, even seemed to be trying to communicate with me in some manner. But no sound whatever reached my consciousness.

"It was a great relief, however, to discover that there was a change taking place, that I was really able to see things. I was amazed at the beings I saw. I could not believe now that I was in the right place, for I could not conceive that I could belong with such wonderful beings. You must understand that a spirit who has arrived at a full

8

understanding of the life here, and who feels the urge to live the life of spirit love and service, such spirit expresses the purity of its character by its outward appearance. Not only the features become wonderfully beautiful, but the garments likewise are glorified. And to my unaccustomed eyes, these spirits about me could not be less than angels from on high. I could not feel I belonged with any such advancement.

"So I wondered and waited. As I watched, I became aware that these glorious shapes were communicating with each other. I studied this over, and as my mind became more active, I realized that hearing must be a spirit power as well as sight. No sooner had I reached this conclusion than I was conscious of sound. And, oh, the sweetness of that first musical tone! Heavenly music indeed! I was entranced! I was in heaven after all! Not only were there beautiful angels, but I surely was going to hear the heavenly choirs!

"It was not long before I could hear spoken words, and then everything was soon explained to me. It was a day of joy; an exhilaration that I probably will never experience again. But there has been no disappointment since. My education was not rapid, but I advanced surely, and I am now experiencing the pleasures that I only faintly glimpsed in the teachings of my earth life.

"When I first became able to understand the spirits about me, I was not sure that I would ever be like one of these wonderful beings; but I did begin to realize that there was opportunity for me to learn more of my new surroundings.

"I was never much of a student on earth and so for a time I was content to enjoy the beautiful scenes about me. I was curious, however, to learn what made the difference in appearance between myself and the others, and my questions were freely answered. I was told that it was necessary for me to work out my own advancement. I was to learn from all sources that appealed to me, and when I decided what I most wished to take up as a study, the rest would be easy.

"I was not interested at first in the work they were doing for the new arrivals. I was too much occupied in using my newly found powers of sight and hearing. I was selfish, of course, in not thinking of all that had been done for me. But I had not been a model of unselfishness on earth, and my character did not change at once. I was gradually drawn to the work of helping others by the fact that several whom I had known on earth came to this side, and my curiosity led me to watch them. It was not long until one of them began to regain consciousness, and I was eager to welcome him and explain to him what I had learned. In this way my work for these new spirits was taken up; and for a long time I did little else.

"I was being slowly educated in spirit life by all that I saw and heard around me. And my inquiring mind finally caused me to realize that there were higher things to learn. I was not much inclined to join any class for study, but I did take time to go to other circles and see what was being done. I had always been interested in music, but was never a musician. It was something I never felt I could master. When I listened to the wonderful music here I was enthusiastic over its beauty. I wondered if it might be possible for me to do anything with it myself. I was led to undertake the study, and I am now progressing slowly.

"You will wonder why I am selected to tell you of my life here, for I have nothing novel to relate. My experience could be duplicated in most ways by thousands of others.

"I was well known on earth, and my name would be recognized by many. I am sure, though, that most of my old friends will be amazed to learn that I have decided to study music. I was a politician on earth, and was more interested in swaying the opinions of other men than in educating any special talent in myself. I was always interested in seeing my political party in power, and bent all my energies toward showing the people that it was the proper remedy for their ills.

"I was not a married man. I lived in an eastern city, and was known as a 'good fellow' there and in other cities where I had occasion to go. I was a traveler to some extent, having visited Europe a number of times. I never held office myself, and was never a candidate. I wonder if you will be able to get my name?"

THE STUDENT

A new personality appeared one evening with questions for us to answer. He proved to be an earnest seeker after information, but his first questions aroused our suspicions as to the sincerity of his inquiries. The whole interview was an entire surprise, and should cause the skeptic to think long and carefully if he is inclined to place the origin in the subconscious mind of the psychic. Such persons always try to make the subconscious mind more wonderful than it really is. Sis took up the pencil with the intent to ask Mary some questions, but there was no wait for them. The pencil began at once:—

"Will you take a message from one who wishes to communicate?"
'Is it any one I know?'
"Will you try to listen to what he says?"
'Is this Mary?'
"Will you try to take his message?"
'Who is writing? Are you any one I know?'
"Will you try to take his words?"
'I want to know who is writing first?'
"He is known here as a student of theosophy and would like to tell you of his conclusions."
'I would like first to know just who you are?'
"Will you be patient while he explains?"
'Are you the ancient spirit who once tried to write?'
"No, I am not the one whom Mary refused to allow. I am a student of many things, and am very much interested in the various beliefs of the future, for even here there is room for different beliefs and creeds. I am not convinced of the ways of the eastern philosophers, yet their reasoning is often eloquent and persuasive. What do you believe is the final condition, the ultimate fate of the soul?"

'We do not believe eastern philosophy, but rather that there is progression on that side as on this, and that progress continues indefinitely.'

"Will that theory be received by logicians, do you think? Will you tell me if many believe in eternal progress? Will you tell me your reasons for believing it?"

'That is what we have been taught from that side, and it appeals to our reason.'

"Is it better than a state of heavenly calm and happiness—Nirvana? Or better even than a return to earth to live out other and higher lives?"

'But we are told that the soul does not return to earth?'

"That is the opinion of many wise ones here. I am asking for the wisdom of the earth mind and desire only."

'Many here believe in reincarnation; but it seems so much more reasonable to us that progress goes on from there, rather than to come back into the sins and sorrows of this world to try to progress. It would seem to offer much more happiness to leave all earthly troubles behind forever.'

"That is admirable, and looks like true happiness; but I wonder if it is the truth?"

'Cannot you find out if it is the truth?'

"I am interested in developing myself by study and by contact with the thoughts and beliefs of others."

"Then why do you not seek the highest teachers there?"

"I shall some time, and will apply myself closely. But at present I am trying to get at some consensus of earth opinion.

'If I were looking for higher things, trying to learn of final conditions, I would not look backward to earth conditions.'

"You do not quite understand me, I am sure, and perhaps it is not necessary. But if one should be a teacher of the progress of life on earth, would he not begin with the lower forms?"

'Are you a teacher?'

"I am trying to prepare myself for a teacher, and I have a certain delight in studying the evolution of belief in the past, and the probable evolution of belief in the future."

'I am still wondering why you do not try to get this from teachers there?'

"Will you believe that I am not a foolish inquirer. I am truly working along the lines I have described. The spirits here have evolved too far to be a beginning of such history, and I have wished to go back to the earth and start at the beginning. You are a long way from the beginning, but yet a link in the great chain of evidence. How I wish I could show you the infinitely subtle and varied changes from age to age, from soul to soul, each age leading a little higher in effort and belief, each age overcoming much of superstition and ignorance. Just now belief and faith on earth are being made so complex by the shadings of philosophy, psychology and other new thought, that it is hard to move on or up in a straight line. But I tell you the study is fascinating, and so you will see it some day.

"You look for an abiding place for your faith. I am studying the different phases or 'abiding places' which have served for millions of years. I am not frivolous, I am interested, and preparing to help others on this side when I can."

'Well, it has seemed to us to be far more satisfactory to go on developing ourselves, our personality, our individuality, continuously on that side, rather than to strive for a state of calm, an eternity of perfection, where one, as Mary has said, would have nothing to do but to contemplate one's own bliss.'

"You have said it! To all of which I say, Amen!"

'Then why are you a student of theosophy?'

"Well, are you not interested sometimes in even heathen rites? I am."

'Yes, certainly, as a matter of history.'

"Well then you can guess the interest I have in this study."

'What is your opinion of the final goal?'

"We are not told definitely. Do you think there would be much of interest in life if every step of the future could be seen? Would not life pall and become uninteresting? We are left much of the old adventurous spirit; we are constantly stimulated with the problems that appear before us. And because the earth people cannot understand, they cavil at the difference of opinion expressed on this side. They do not know that because of the freedom of thought and study on this side our lives are full of tremendous interest. To learn! To know! To choose the wisest and best! That is life!"

A year or two later we asked again for this writer or student. He was sent for and wrote:—

"I am here and glad to come. What do you wish me to talk about?"

'It has been a long time since you talked to us. What have you been doing meantime?'

"You may well ask what I have found of interest in that time. The year has been fruitful of all things that make for progress and knowledge. I have gone on with my efforts to study the philosophies of different minds and peoples."

'Have you been long in the spirit world?'

"Not many years, but they have meant much, meant more than a lifetime on earth."

'We have been reading articles in the magazines that are rather disheartening to one who looks at the spiritual side of things. Scientists are busy supporting material doctrines in so many cases.'

"They have about reached the limit in their particular line of reasoning. Science and scientific investigation seem to develop a high degree of intellect, but they lose out on the spiritual side. Now, the belief here is that as all of this investigation fails to account for life and progress—infinite progress, eternal progress—they will finally, as a last resort, turn to the spiritual side of life again.

"Somewhere in the mind and soul of man is the unsatisfied longing for a greater perfection of life and character, a desire for something beyond the fevered struggle for mortal existence; something to rest upon. And through this desire the spiritual side of life is bound to awaken. It is the thought here, and we wait confidently for man himself to demand this last and highest evolution."

Referring to the magazine articles again, we said that some of the writers seemed to think that religion was just a passing phase.

"Religion is a phase, but is the highest phase, and *will not pass away.* The germ of this religious longing existed in the life principle, and has kept pace with man up through his whole career; not always wise, not always even spiritual, as the pagans have shown, but always the longing for something higher and better. This is the God-given part of evolution."

'It is difficult to convince some.'

"The convincing part will come of itself eventually, for it is inherent in the soul."

'Our fear is that so many are ready for an excuse to turn away from any spiritual demand, ready to make the most of a material existence, that all morality will be destroyed?'

"That tendency will destroy morality if it conquers the world. But *it will not conquer!* We here know that, and already see the signs of a higher thought and the rebirth of spirituality. Forces are at work on both sides here, but a higher force than either will finally conquer."

'A few here believe that, and also profess to believe that a spiritual leader will soon arise?'

"Not as a Messiah, but as a spiritual awakening and a joining of that life to this: the study and practice of drawing near to us, and of finding the proof of this life over and over again, and the education spiritually that will come from this phase."

We spoke of the discouragements that appeared in so many ways.

"You must stop measuring and stop doubting! Give the truth to the world as you see it, and let this truth do its own work.

"Do not worry. It will all come about at last. Study evolution as I have done and see the slow growth of character and knowledge throughout uncounted ages, and comfort yourself with the belief that you are putting a thought here and there, planting it like a seed which will spring up and bring a larger harvest than you imagine.

"We see the increase in wickedness and crime, and we grieve over the chaos. We know of the cruelties there, but we also see the tenderness that is given to those who have come through the shadows to us—we mean the innocent sufferers from earth's cruelty. As to the criminals: be sure their crimes must find atonement before they can come into happiness. Justice is a big word, but it is the foundation of kindness.

"We do not look upon the world as you do. The hopelessness, as it seems to you there, is illumined by our knowledge here, and our unfaltering faith in the powers of good. We believe in God, in all and through all and overall. And we have proof of His existence that you cannot have there. We never doubt the final outcome. But the way is long, and at present filled with pitfalls and darkness to the eyes of mortals. Do not fear! Work as you can, and trust for the rest."

THE PARTNERS

When our leaders on the other side were away one evening, the time was filled by another member of their circle who wrote through my pencil as follows:—

"We would like to tell of our experiences, as they are a little out of the ordinary. We are two who were associated in business in earth life. We were in a western city not far from Chicago. We were not very well educated, but had many years of business experience, and had always been together. We were not interested in books or reading of any kind, except the items of local interest, and occasional articles that were concerned with business. We talked a good deal with people whom we met, and were, I think, considered intelligent.

"We were church members, but not active; attended occasionally when our families were persuasive enough. We gave no thought to a future life, just lived a day-to-day existence. We were not wealthy, but always had plenty to make us feel comfortable. We both had automobiles, and liked to ride when opportunity offered, which was usually on Sunday.

"It so happened one Sunday that few from our families wished to ride, so four of us were in my automobile including my friend and partner. We miscalculated at a railroad crossing and we two soon found ourselves on this side. That is, we left our earthly bodies. Here is where our unusual experience comes in.

"We had just been laughing and talking about an article in the paper concerning ghosts. After our spirits left our bodies, we each seemed to realize that an accident had occurred, but each thought himself uninjured. But each could see the spirit form of the other, and its peculiar appearance to his new powers of spirit sight convinced him that his partner had been killed and that his ghost was still present. It was a 'Comedy of Errors,' if ever there was one,—right in the midst of tragedy. Each thinking himself in the flesh and the other a ghost, there was no attempt to speak, so the mistake was not discovered.

"After the first excitement was over we seemed to drift into oblivion for a time, and we think it must have been some months before we were aware that we were alive only in spirit. During that time we were separated. We were quite slow in gaining our knowledge of what had happened. Our experiences were not just the same, but nearly so. I think the realization that I had died probably came to me the earlier. When I did realize this I was so filled with despair at leaving my earthly existence, and so little used to spirit ways, that all thought of my partner was absent for a long time. It seems his experience was slightly different. At any rate, he thought of me, and at once began to search for me. Because of our close companionship he soon found me, and we have started on the road together.

"We had a hearty laugh over our ghostly experience, but also mingled with sorrow for our families left behind, two of whom were badly injured at the time we were killed. But as time passes, and we learn of the beauties and joys of this life, we realize that we have lost our desire to really return to earth life, and we anticipate now the things that we may attain in the future."

EARTHQUAKE VICTIMS

"We are not Mary and Dee. We are friends who wish to find friends on earth."

'Is Mary there?'

"Not now; but she is willing that we should write. When she comes she will tell you that she has given us permission."

Mary, our leader on that side, usually guards the writing very carefully to prevent undeveloped or malicious spirits from bothering.

"We wish to know if anyone has survived the great catastrophe which brought us over?"

Sis had been reading about recent mine disasters in the papers, and naturally this was in her mind. But the pencil went on, quite away from that thought:—

"We were killed in the earthquake in Japan, and so many came, we wonder if any were left?"
'Were you Japanese?'
"We were Americans, resident in Yokohama. We came as suddenly as if shot out of a cannon. I cannot describe the awfulness. We were not the first to come, and so had the terror, the horrible scenes of prevailing death, before we ourselves were killed."
'How were you killed?'

18

"Falling walls, opening ground, and tidal waves all seemed to combine for the one unendurable moment in which we found our destruction. Then all was blank, all silence; knowledge faded, fear departed, leaving a sense of deep and quiet rest."

This seems to us to give in a few words a wonderful picture of the moment of death.

'Do you know the response the United States made for help?'

And Sis related some of the things that were done.

"That is like the U.S.A., all one way or all the other! Will they now be at peace with Japan, I mean in the true sense of neighborliness?"
'I am afraid the old color prejudice is too strong.'
"We too had some of that same prejudice when there. But, ah! if you could only see their white souls now! You would grieve over the blindness that refused to recognize them in their earth life!

"We have one message to give: that we live, and that each is going to his or her 'own place.' For not all souls are white, not all are risen above selfishness, not all were kind instead of cruel, not all put service in place of self-seeking."

Mary came at this moment, and wrote:—

"This is a true message. We know of the long and patient endeavor of their guardians to bring them out of their mortal condition of terror and pain."

A SPIRIT FROM EARLIEST TIMES

"There is someone here who would like to write. We will help him to say what he wishes. He says:—

"I am of another country and another language, but we here can translate our thought into your earth form of words.

"I wish most of all to have you believe in us, for we are trying mightily to influence the earth people heavenward. You see and know a little of the wickedness there, the heartless cruelty of a few, the dishonesty of many, and the paralyzing power of materialism against spiritual advance.

"What can we do? For the materialistic mind is not open to spirit influence. Therefore we try to find some medium of approach through other souls and minds, that we may in some way pierce the shell of materialistic thought. You are many times discouraged because of the growth and power of evil-mindedness there; and we here are only kept from discouragement by the knowledge that the right must prevail, for this is the law of the heavenly universe. No matter how slow the planets seem to move, their course is uninterrupted; no matter how slowly the great wheel of evolution turns, it still revolves and brings righteousness to all. But that event, that "far-off divine event," comes with a slowness that we feel as well as you. Now can you and will you help us to get our words over?

"You wish to know who I am. I lived long ago in an age far more engulfed in wickedness than the present one; and I shuddered at what I saw, felt, and could not alter, and kept silent, knowing that words meant death."

'You must have lived in the Greek or Roman times?'

"Before that even, when there was no light, no spiritual light on earth."

'In Babylon?'

"No, before that. When you read in history of ancient times, traditions, sacrifices to strange gods, human sacrifices, and no one to tell us of a higher or better way, you read of the time when I lived, when

20

I was a part of the great earthborn multitude. Only that deep down in my subconscious self there was an instinctive feeling that there was something better, something purer and brighter and higher than the life that was lived."

'Can you tell us where this was?'

"Over in Asia. But even the names are changed now. It was a land that knew not the true God, a land in which worship was ever cruelty. I came over because of cruelty, for I myself was a sacrifice to the gods! Can you believe this?"

'It is certainly a strange story!'

Mary says, "Listen to him, for it is true. We know his history and know he is telling the truth; and the story can be multiplied by thousands of experiences."

'Why have they not advanced in all the ages?'

"He has advanced. He is from a higher plane. But his desire to help the earth people enables him to come back to conditions in which he can communicate with them."

A SPIRIT FROM THE TIME OF CROMWELL

"We think the earth people should be made thoroughly acquainted with what is in store for them here. It is not always happiness at first, and for some it seems that unhappiness is their lot for a very long time; and all because of too firmly fixed ideas of what the future is like.

"We have in mind one who has been under our direct care for a time. He is now a happy and joyous soul, but it seems that he has been here for generations, and all that time he has been in a purgatory of his own making.

21

"He was an Englishman, and left the earth in the time of Cromwell. He was a religious enthusiast, and had pictured the future life in terms of hellfire on the one hand, and ages of bliss on the other. Not finding either, he conceived the idea that he had somehow missed the way, and was condemned to everlasting solitude. Can you understand what torment this would bring?"

'But in those times, was he to blame for having such ideas?'

For the moment it seemed to us a terribly unjust punishment.

"We feel that he should have been able to learn more clearly what earth justice was, and that would have made him a different sort of a man. But he was opposed to anything contrary to his beliefs, and was unjust and oppressive to all who held them. This was something he should have been able to overcome despite his heredity and environment. We know that many who lived at that time had right ideas of justice, and administered the law with love and mercy. Such cases should have been an example for this man to follow. But he held the idea that only his way would take one into the realms of bliss in the future life, and he vigorously opposed any other belief."

'Was not that Cromwell's idea?'

"Yes, and he was many years in learning the truth here. But being a man of greater intelligence and reason, he did learn the truth sooner than the other one. But after all, he only saw there the same justice and injustice that the other man saw."

'But for so many, heredity and environment seem to positively hedge about all their actions and ideas?'

"Yes, of course we were not all cast in the same mold. But we were all given the power of reason and choice. Unfortunately, too many set themselves up as judges, and fail to observe the arguments on the other side.

22

"We think these things should be given a thorough study by the earth people. If the consequences here could be fully shown, they would certainly make some of them stop and examine themselves to ascertain what road they were traveling.

"When we were trying to influence this man we found that he was only able to move from place to place, and to see dimly some of his surroundings. He was not able to see those who were trying to help him, and he could hear nothing. His own thoughts were all the company he had through the long centuries. We do not know just how long the time seemed to him, for of course he had no way of measuring it. But he says he can only express it by saying that it seemed endless.

"We were able to influence him by surrounding him with music. The continuous tones at last broke through his deafness, and set him to wondering whence they came. His attention having once been drawn to the fact that he was receiving impressions of sound, he was then led to detect other sounds, and finally made to understand that someone was trying to talk to him. After that the progress was rapid."

THE SMALL MERCHANT

"You have my sympathy if I am to write for you, for I am a new hand at this business, and fear I will not make much of a success of it. We are glad to have the opportunity to write when your leaders are not here, for they have more important things to say, and our little chatter has to wait.

"I am not a newcomer to this side of life, but I am rather new in this circle. I am trying to become familiar with the work of writing, for I am told I have much psychic power, and if I can become proficient in the use of this power, I may be of some service to others who have more important things to tell you.

"I was a man on earth who thought he was living a pretty good sort of life. I did not gamble, or do dishonest things, in the little business which I conducted. But I was not much interested in other people, and I see now that many times I was hard and selfish, when it would have been so easy to be kind and generous instead.

"Life there is looked upon as a sort of grab game. He who is most skillful in grabbing is supposed to be the most successful. Not necessarily a dishonest practice, but surely a selfish one. I was not situated where I could seize anything of any great value, but where the odds allowed it, I saw that they fell on my side.

"I was a small merchant in a small town. I was successful in a small way, but I made of myself a small man personally. And when I came here and learned what this life meant, it was a very small niche that I occupied for a very long time.

"I am growing slowly, and am trying to overcome the habits formed during my long life there. I have reached a point where I feel that these handicaps are more imagined than real now. So I make light of them and try to be happy.

"It is a wonderful world here. It is a wonderful life that is open to everyone. I feel sometimes that I do not deserve all the opportunities that lie before me. But I will try to be worthy of a little of the happiness that comes to me, and I will endeavor to send back to earth a little of the knowledge I am acquiring.

"When you come you will be able to see the results of selfishness in nearly every soul that comes, and will see that many have the feeling of being in the wrong place because unprepared. I was so unprepared that I did not even know that I was still alive for a long time. It was a surprise to learn the truth, and it was a hard road I had to travel."

A WOMAN's EXPERIENCE

"I have watched the writing many times and have wondered if my experience would add anything to your records that you would find interesting.

"I am a woman. I have been here many years. I was born and brought up on the Atlantic coast, and moved to one of your western states when I was married. But that was many years ago. The year was 1840. I lived a lonely life on a farm, had many hardships; raised a family; and finally left my weary existence at the age of 68. I was never a church member, although brought up by Puritan parents. In coming into the western country I brought none of that teaching with me, however. In some ways I think I would have been happier if I had, for I would at least have been looking forward to something after death. As it was, I was so weary of life, I looked forward to peace and nothingness. I was ready to give up everything, there was so little I cared for.

"When I finally realized that death had not ended my existence, I did not know what to make of it. I could see or hear nothing. But I knew I was alive and that I had left my earthly body. I was distracted. For I felt that now I could not rid myself of life, no matter how much I suffered, or how weary I was. But I soon found that I was not suffering, except from loneliness, and after a time I began to wonder what it all meant. Surely there was something I had failed to understand. I certainly was not meant to pass through eternity in this lonely condition. Somewhere, somehow, I would meet someone in like condition, and then we could talk it over and try to arrive at some understanding.

"By good fortune my mind was so undeveloped at that time that I did not have very bright reasoning powers, so time itself did not seem so long as it might. But I did finally reason that if I met someone and wanted to talk, I would have to make this person understand by new means. It seems that this thought of itself brought some light

25

and understanding. For it was not long before I was aware that I was beginning to see and hear faintly. It was a delight, you may be sure, and you on earth can never conceive the joy I experienced when I first realized that someone was trying to talk with me. Of course it was not long then until I was taught how to use my spirit powers, and soon I was able to take up my new life. In contrast with my old one anything would have brought joy. But if I could make you comprehend even one small portion of the reality, you would still be far from realizing my full happiness.

"This is all. It isn't much. But it may help someone poor soul there to understand, and I do so want all there to know the happiness that awaits them here."

THE NEWCOMER

"We have brought a newcomer to talk to you tonight. He has come quickly into consciousness, and into understanding of his spirit powers, and we thought you would like to hear what his first impressions are. We will write for him, as he is not able to do that yet."

"I have not been here long, and have lost none of my interest in the affairs of mortal existence. It is a wonderful change, and my mind has been so filled with the new sights and scenes, the new phases of existence, that I have not had time to be lonely.

"I have learned one thing already that it seems to me the earth people should be told. It is that *we cannot change our character at the moment of death*. What we have made of ourselves during our earth life determines what we will be here to a very large extent. I suppose one who was malicious or criminal there will in time change his character here: but the characteristics which caused him to turn to an evil life there will be his strong characteristics here; and he will have to learn how to turn these to better use.

26

"I think this point is not at all realized on earth. Those who believe the Bible teachings are too often filled with the idea that repentance will remake them, no matter what kind of a life they have lived. And those who do not have this idea are usually lacking in *any* conclusion on the subject.

"I think I would also like to tell the earth people that it is not hard to pass through the gates of death. I found nothing that should cause any dread, and I am told that there should be no fear by anyone.

"I wish I had powers of description sufficient to tell you of my impressions of the life here. I do not know how human language can ever adequately express the beauty and charm of it all.

"I was met by my guides, and by those who were sent to help me, and I am thankful to say that I was soon made to understand the things necessary for me to do. I was soon able to see and hear, and not long in learning how to express myself. I was very slow at times on earth to grasp the meaning of spiritual things, but I was honest and earnest, and always seeking knowledge. I had formed no very definite ideas of this life, but I did have a firm belief that personality continued. I was not ill long, so I arrived with little loss of vigor, and with little to unlearn. I realize that I was extremely fortunate, for I see so many who have much difficulty in understanding what this life means.

"I was fortunate too in finding this circle, for it contains some rarely beautiful souls; and for their companionship alone, heaven is a wonderful place. I am told there are many equally delightful circles, but I also know there are many spirits who cling together because of similar ideas and beliefs who lack much in advancement.

"So I find my pathway broad and easy, and my life one of continuous delight. I have taken up no studies of importance yet, and may not do so for a time. To observe, and learn by observing, seem sufficient just now.

"I know your teachers, Mary and Dee, and as they are not here, I can express myself freely as to the loveliness and beauty of their souls. No finer are in heaven, I am sure. I will not stray far from these wonderful people, so you may hear from me again as I wander to and fro."

Then one of the circle wrote:—

"He is one in a million. We think he should have been a famous man on earth, but for some reason which we have not learned, he seems to have been known there only to a small community. But we all know he was a great influence there. We are pleased to have him with us."

THE STORY OF THE SCHOOL TEACHER

"We are anxious to tell you our story. It is a little different from most you have, and may interest someone there.

"I was a schoolteacher on earth in a western village. I worked hard, almost starved at times in order to buy the other things I craved. I was never married, and had little attention from the male sex. I was not old when death relieved me from further efforts to keep body and soul together.

"The one who is my companion now was a man much above me in intellectual station when he was on earth. He was a college graduate, a successful teacher, and had a comfortable living. He too remained unmarried. We met here soon after his arrival, as I was caring for some of the newcomers. I was attracted to him by his undoubted culture; and when he was able to understand this life he seemed drawn to me by the fact that learning and knowledge meant so much to me. I was not then ready to form an alliance, for I had never felt any necessity for such a partner. So we drifted along. I went on with my work of helping the poor souls who came in such multitudes with every passing day. When I next met my friend he had climbed high in the study of astronomy, which you know is one of the fascinating attractions here. I was induced to join him in one of the excursions for observation, and during the journey my inner self began to realize the need for a more constant companionship with someone. And after our return I allowed the intimacy to grow. It soon ripened into the great attraction that draws all of opposite sex together at some time in their journey through eternity.

"We have been together now for a long time, and the bliss of close companionship is what I would somehow like to tell you about so that the world can get some faint understanding of this part of our life and happiness. But how can I tell it! It is the most wonderful experience of one's life, as those on earth know who have had the good fortune to realize it there.

"We see many who come here who have thought they had made an alliance which would last forever, who had no real conception of such happiness. It is felt only once by anyone, and can never be mistaken when it really comes. I have watched the growth of several such attractions here, and I realize that the earth life seldom encounters the real thing. Many married people continue together here for a long time, and yet gradually drift apart as they learn the true laws governing such matings. It is always happiness, however. Such separations here are never accompanied with sorrow.

"It may seem a little indelicate to you for me to enlarge upon so intimate a subject. But we here know that it is the ultimate happiness of everyone, and something which most here are ready to take into consideration at any time. If you will remember who is writing this, you will find when you come two of the happiest souls whom you will have the pleasure to meet. But it is always so, isn't it? All lovers think their case is the very best the world ever saw or knew. We here know, of course, that it is only a question of temperament and character that determines the depth of the happiness that comes with each mating. But for those concerned there is never any other that compares with theirs.

"Well, I will not gush any further on the subject. But I felt that this would be something I could write easily about, and we know you are seeking the full truth of this life."

DIFFERENT VIEWPOINTS

"We have our different personalities here as we did there, and we do not all look at things in the same way here anymore than we did there. If you can receive the ideas of many from here it will aid you in forming a more correct understanding. If you only have one person's messages you only get their viewpoint and their way of expressing it. I have been here many years as earth time goes, and I have myself seen fit to change my ideas about some things more than once, as I obtained a fuller understanding of them.

"We know that there are certain fundamental truths, just as you know there are certain fundamental laws. But in the various things which surround these truths there are matters which we can interpret according to the impressions they make upon us. We might use as an example the attitude that most of us take here in regard to the union of the two sexes. When I first came over I was thoroughly convinced that there was no marriage in heaven, and for a long time I could not see that there was anything to indicate it. I saw men and women associating freely and independently, and although I saw apparent friendships of more than usual intensity, I did not think of them as inseparable. If I had been communicating with earth at that time I would have conscientiously said that there was no mating here that was lasting. But now I know that the two sexes are drawn together here some time by indissoluble ties. And of such is the Kingdom of Heaven.

"I might also tell of the first ideas I had regarding the way children grow and reach maturity. I saw children occasionally, and I saw teachers instructing them at times. But I did not understand that they grew up here just as they do there, only more rapidly. I thought they always remained children; and I associated some of them with the ideas I had on earth of 'cherubs.' It was really quite an astonishment when I did learn the truth. I could hardly believe it, so firmly fixed were my first ideas.

"In matters of a more abstract nature I see I am even now not in entire agreement with many fine advanced spirits. We have minds to reason with, and when certain facts are given us we use them according to our own personality, just as two carpenters will build different houses out of the same materials.

"I could give you many examples. In caring for the newcomers, I have different views from many. But I have succeeded and they have succeeded, so who is right?

"You may think that I am something of a freak, perhaps, but I can assure you that I am not unique. We find much pleasure here in the fact that we do have different personalities and different ideas. It makes life more enjoyable in every way. If we all thought alike we should necessarily all be alike, and we most of us think we prefer variety."

After he ceased, our leader remarked:—

"We like him very much. He is not eccentric, just a strong character, one who believes firmly what his mind reasons out as the truth. We think that is what the mind is for, so we think such individuals are showing the greatest progress."

THE ORDINARY BUSINESSMAN

"I was never given to mysteries, I was just a plain ordinary businessman, trying to take care of my wife and family, and keep them from want, in either intellectual or physical ways. My sons went through college, my daughters to a boarding school, and I thought I had done pretty well by them all. But I did not bring them up in any spiritual thought: I left them to find what they could from church

31

or books or papers. They are there yet, a worldly set, living only a material life. What can I do for them now? Is there any help?"

'Could you reach any of them through influence from there?'

"I think not. None of us thought of spirit life, none of us tried for silent influence or silent cultivation. In fact, we did not know the term. We thought all education was for the brain, and then to react in business or pleasure. The consequence is that I have been a long, long time in arriving at anything here that I could call happiness. And I want to preach a sermon to my family; *and I cannot!*

"What influence is there on earth which could guide them to a quicker realization of the happiness here?"

'The church *should* be able to do it.'

"I doubt if it does. Too formal; and my boys and girls were not much of churchgoers anyway."

I said there were good books if only they and the readers could be brought together.

"Mary says, that is the trouble. The public generally frowns on spirit communications or spirit belief. The church is good, and for many, their salvation. Yet its formal doctrines and observances do not always educate toward the highest spiritual life.

"No, he will simply have to wait until they arrive here. He himself has outgrown all of the earthborn creeds, and looks, as we do, to the Supreme Power and Love for inspiration and guidance. All will be well with his family at last, but they will come slowly into the higher life because we judge from what he has told us, they are absorbed in purely worldly social plans, and have little or no thought of this life."

SEEKING EARTH FRIENDS

Mary and Dee were called away one evening, and the other members of the circle explained their absence.

"They were called to another circle to help find an earth friend for a spirit lately arrived. They have done so much of this work, they are frequently called to other circles.

"They have succeeded when others have failed, many times, in aiding newly arrived spirits, and in helping others who are here. For there are many unanswered questions for those who first arrive. Sometimes they expect to find the heavenly home as they themselves have constructed it from Bible references or Sunday sermons or funeral descriptions; and they become dazed and halfway lost because they do not find this heaven of their imagination.

"There is much to do here to help the multitudes who come. With every second some soul arrives on this side. Sometimes in great catastrophes they arrive by hundreds. Can you not see how often we are called to help? Everyone is tenderly cared for. Some are worthy, some are unworthy. But they are received gently and lovingly in every case."

A friend had asked if we could find a relative on that side for him. We apparently succeeded, but there was a little doubt of the identity, both because he came so quickly, and because his remarks were not as expected. We inquired if they thought masquerading?

"We can always tell when the truth is not told. There is a peculiar clouding of the form and appearance. So far as we could tell, he was the one the messenger sought.

"We wish we could explain this phase of life to you more definitely. It is not easy for strangers to come and to talk freely. Some succeed, others do not. It is a great hindrance to the acceptance of many messages from here. We have told you of many of the difficulties of communication, but you will never fully understand until you come.

"We have no doubt that this was the one for whom you were inquiring. He was excited over the prospect of talking, and was much disappointed that he could not get through more easily.

"He came quickly, as you say. We sent messengers, and they seemed to find him at once. You must understand that the service is very complete, much more so than any telegraph or radio that has been invented. We do not always find them so quickly, of course, for sometimes they are far away, or in some work they cannot leave, or are not advanced, or sometimes even, have gone on to higher planes. But this time the one sought was evidently not far away.

"We are glad to bring friends to you, and hope you can understand some of the difficulties we have to overcome."

At another time this spirit did succeed in writing, and the following is a part:—

"You know I did not believe as you did. I thought—if I thought at all—along the lines the church had laid out. I do not remember much of my coming: I seemed to finally drop into a peaceful sleep. How long, I do not know. Then a new consciousness seemed to come slowly. There was beauty about me; people moving; music far away, but beautiful. But I supposed the music must be from harps played by angels. Old ideas are strong, you know.

"Then I found I could move. I saw a wonderful shining form near me—my guide, I afterwards learned—and, strangely enough, I felt acquainted with this stranger! He took me by the hand, or so it seemed, and together we explored this wonderful new country. Patient with all my ignorance, wise when I was foolish, tender when I was almost afraid; but through it all, he was leading, guiding me through wonderful scenes, and bringing me to a trust, a happiness and well-being, I never knew before.

"This was my first experience of the new life. Afterward came the desire to fit myself into the wonderful surroundings; and studies were suggested. Studies? Why, pleasures, I should say! For thought is so quick here that study is the wrong name.

"Then came moving from place to place, growing acquainted with other spirits. And though I have not risen very high in heavenly learning, I am thrilled with new power and look forward to an eternity of knowledge, growth and happiness."

MYSTICISM

"We know that many people cannot think of this life unless in terms of wonder and ecstasy. It seems that all who have had visions of this world have been so overwhelmed with its beauty, that they picture it to others in terms that make it appear far different from the reality. They have caught the beauty and glory, but have not sensed the reasonableness, the orderliness, the harmony.

"We believe that a mystery is necessary to attract some minds. They are not satisfied with the trials and commonplace circumstances of the earth life, and feel that heaven to be satisfactory, must have the wonders, the glory, that not only surpass any of earth life, but must surpass all understanding. It is unfortunate, because such an attitude is not conducive to an acceptance of many of the truths of this life.

"We wish we could make the world understand that heaven is not so unlike the earth existence. It is *beautiful*, it is even wonderful. But along with its attractions in that way, there are joys that compare with those of earth in their ability to thrill those who experience them, yet joys that come from experiences here not unlike many that occur in earth associations.

"We believe we have made this plain in the messages we have sent over, and we hope they can be placed before the world. We know there are things in this life that warrant some of the ideas that are held there. But we have not yet arrived at the conditions where these are experienced. Life advances slowly. No great changes come in a moment. Even death is found not to be the wonderful transition that many expect. Growth, always growth, is the law of life everywhere. We will have mysteries to solve in due time, but they will not be put before us until we can have the knowledge and wisdom that will enable us to master them.

"It is to us an illogical way of looking at this life. For if the glories and mysteries were so profound, it would necessitate a miracle for their solution by the newcomer—a capacity and experience that no one would naturally possess. If given to the spirit in a moment, it would of necessity so change his personality as to make him a new individual.

"We see many here who still cling to such ideas, and usually they are slow in understanding this life. It is so different from what they expected, that they are unable to recognize it as heaven at all."

A CASE OF OBSESSION

The following is given with Miss Dresser's introduction: The experience recorded below has touched me more deeply than I can well express. A. H. was my playmate as a child, and my companion in girlhood. She was particularly bright and attractive, but her lack of reverence and the absence of anything like spirituality had not then appeared to the degree that was manifested later. The record gives the rest of the story.

"We will bring someone to talk to you. Whom do you wish?"

'Oh, some of my old friends.'

"We think the old ones will suit your mood tonight. Whom shall it be?"

'Someone I can quarrel with. How about Mr. S or Dr. B? I used to have many discussions with them in the way I refer to as 'quarreling.''

Sis naturally expected one or both these old friends, as it is usual for them to bring the one for whom we ask. Then this was written:—

"I am here. Who am I? I am not the ones you asked for, but am one of your oldest friends, who might pick a quarrel with you if you are looking for variety."

Entirely in the dark as to who this was, Sis asked:—

    'Did I ever quarrel with you?'
    "Yes, truly you did."

Sis guessed several without success, and then said she could not remember anyone who might answer the description.

"You did know me, surely; though I was never sure of your liking me."

Sis asked if it had been in either of several cities in which she had lived, and finally if in her own home town.

"Yes; though you were not there all the time."

    'I don't believe I know you.'
    "*You do!*"

She guessed several more without success. Then as a last resort, but absolutely unbelieving, she asked if it were A. H., and was astounded when the pencil wrote an emphatic—

"Yes!"

'I don't believe it!'

"I am here; and I have found out what was the matter with me. *I was possessed by a devil! There now!*"

This old friend had died in an insane asylum some years before and Sis could hardly believe that it was she.

"I have been asleep for a long time, and when I waked, it was with horror as I was shown a picture of what I had been. My poor sister! How I hated her! Hate! Hate! Hate! Everyone and everything!

"You will not believe any good of me now, I am afraid, but truly, I am my own early self. Never very angelic, never much good, but always hoping I would be good some time."

'When did the obsession begin?'

"I think the beginning was after I went west. I don't know exactly, but the influence did not possess me all at once. First I seemed to think unkind thoughts of people. Then I grew to criticizing them, saying and thinking hard and ugly things. Then of course I lost the love and respect of the friends I had had. Oh, how that evil spirit must have laughed to see its power over me! From worse to worse I went, until I hated my own dear ones; and I suspect even now I have not been shown my worst.

"I have had a spirit guide, I am told, but this guide could not protect me, because I never looked spiritward. You remember that I was never religious. I never prayed, nor even thought spirit thoughts. I wanted a good time, and many times I succeeded in getting them. I would not go to church; many things in church seemed funny to me instead of serious. Oh, I can see it all now, and how this natural disposition made it difficult for my own guide to reach me. How could it be otherwise, when I made fun of all religious thought? Then, as my guide could not protect me, the evil spirit saw the open way to my life, to my inner consciousness, and by degrees took possession. I did not recognize the evil, and so became an easy victim.

"But now you must believe in me and in the change. I did not feel sure of anything except my own rage at life and everyone connected with it. But I'll try now to make amends for some of the things.

"But, oh, how easy it is to be good here where there is no physical weakness, where there is no discord, where love is the law of life! I never knew what heaven was like. If only the ministers would tell their people of the love and thoughtfulness here, of the naturalness of this life, with its continuous unbroken kindness and *no hell*, except what we make for ourselves, the world would be saved.

"Why don't you tell them?"

'You mean the public?'

"Yes. Why not?"

'They have been told many times, but they will not believe.'

"No! Is that so? Well, I suppose they will have to be born again before they can know the reality of this life."

'It seems so. Most people do not seem to want to hear about it.'

"Well, we must wait, then, until they come here. We can help a little, can we not?"

'Do you wish to help?'

"*Yes! I want to help!*"

'Do you know Dee?'

"Yes, and she is lovely. She was the one who kept the secret from you until I was ready to talk. I could not express myself at first. But she knew, and waited for me to be ready. We are so glad of her presence. But how you must miss her!"

'We do. But we know there are many compensations. Have you seen your father and mother?'

"They are here with me, and the happiest people I ever saw. We are together now, and though I will be in this circle, my home will be with them.

"We go now. Love and love and more love, in place of that old hatred. Oh, how *could* that have been!"

'Do they not tell you to forget all that?'

"Yes, they do. But it haunts me,—I mean the memory of it,—yet. I can never be obsessed again, that I know. I realize their power and I know their black deeds. Besides, I am so filled with all the kind and loving thought and service that I see about me, that I could not harbor an evil thought. *And this is heaven*! A heaven as far beyond what I imagined as the stars are above the sea."

Later she wrote again:—

"I am here again, dear friend, and more glad than you can imagine that I may come. I never realized that heaven was so dear. Why! It is like a perfectly beautiful, natural life on earth, if earthly people could ever attain such goodness and beauty! I always wanted to be beautiful, and never realized before, that while we are still on earth, we may be creating beauty that will last into eternity. I am not beautiful yet, don't think that! Too much of the old selfishness left. But I will get rid of it, I know I will! How could I remain selfish, with such surrounding love and unselfishness? Why can't earth people know what is here?"

"You might answer that question. They will not seek that life, or try to know its conditions."

"I know, for I was one of them."

And again:—

"I wish I could give you some idea of the beauty of this life. I never dreamed it could be so different from earth life, and yet so natural. It is perhaps the human life, with the wrongdoing and wrong-thinking eliminated, and all the pure, good and kindly nature left. I never understood it while on earth, and I am wondering now how I can make others understand. If the world *could* know, if it could realize, all would be well and sin forever discarded."

'Mary and Dee are trying to spread the truth.'

"Yes, they are. But the trouble is, they reach only those who are already good and kind."

'The others will not listen.'

40

"That is the trouble. Unkind thought, cruel thought and action, nearly kill the soul—strangle it, I guess—so it cannot ever influence the life."

'What are you trying to do there?'

"I am hoping to be a teacher of some sort, I don't know just how. Probably to help those who come over unprepared, even as I was helped. But I am not ready for that yet."

"Do you remember N. W.?"

"Yes, and I have seen her. She is a wonderful spirit, pure white all the way through."

'Do you mean that metaphorically?'

"Yes, both ways; because the spirit shows externally here, and a white soul will have a pure external; not always white, but a shining and beautiful garment. We wish you could see Mary and Dee. They are lovely in dress as in soul, for the outer garment here is sure to express the inner nature."

'Mary has been described to us as dressed in silvery white?'

"She is often dressed in that way; and your Dee has most wonderful garments. A Parisian dressmaker would be enchanted. But he would try in vain to reproduce such beauty. It is the soul that shines through, and the life that expresses itself in the outer garment.

"I haven't much of a wardrobe yet. I'll hope for a white dress by the time you come."

'What color have you now?'

"A mixed color; some white, but other colors mixed in. I have not overcome my mortal faults or thoughts entirely. But I am trying, *I am!*"

'What do the men wear?'

"They wear a sort of flowing robe, like the classic robes of the Greeks, I think, a little, and these take on the colors of the character too."

Some months later:—

"Here I am again, you see. For Mary lets me come when you are writing because she knows how dear the earth words are to me yet."

41

'What are you doing now?'

"Studying, of course. I'll have to study for a long time before I can begin to help others much. But I do see how each and everyone begins their beautiful life here, just by kindness and constant thoughtfulness for others. Never a selfish thought. Think of it! And I was so selfish!"

'Your sister says you were not.'

"No, that is her love. I was selfish. But I did not realize how terribly I had developed that characteristic. It begins so gradually, so in little things, and grows and grows, until like a horrid weed, it crowds out every kindly sentiment. I know it now, and that is how I came to fall into obsession. If I had lived differently I could have resisted the malicious influence."

Some weeks later we were looking over the above record, and Sis asked if A. H. were there.

"We will call her."

After a few moments her hand and arm were almost violently shaken and it was some moments before it was quiet enough to write. There was evident much excitement behind the influence.

"I am here, and so glad to be called, I could not write quietly."

Sis spoke of our thought to use her experiences, and asked if it would be all right.

"Yes, of course! Do let me help somebody now, if possible. I was such a drag on my sister that I want to help any way and all ways."

'Are you happy?'

"Yes, happier than I ever believed could be possible. I do not quite know how to explain it; but think of a body that is never sick, never tired, and more full of life and pleasure than in the brightest hours on earth. Then imagine, if you can, the perfect peace and affection and unselfishness which are the laws of life here. Then imagine new studies, new opportunities, new surprises, all delightful ones, and a general companionship that fulfills every law of friendship. Then try to be sad or selfish, if you can! *I can't!* Even with the remnants of my old human temper."

There was little hesitancy on Sis's part as to whether she would write more. But the pencil went on:—

"May I write a little more?"

'Why, bless your heart! Certainly!'

"It seems so good to come to my earth friends."

'What are you doing by this time?'

"Studying, I guess, only it seems like play, it is so easy. Oh, you don't know yet the ease with which we can advance in learning. We are supposed to have left our brains in the coffin along with our bodies. But something has taken the place, and of such infinite improvement, I cannot describe it. Only there is no effort in acquiring knowledge—you just want it, and it comes! You will never know a thousandth part of this life, for all the pages and pages and pages that have been written, until you come. Then, oh, then! Happiness and more happiness.

"Well, never mind anything more now. I know you are ready to have me go. Goodbye."

VARIOUS MESSAGES

The selections which are given here are taken from our records to show the various viewpoints of the many communicators who have talked with us. These are only a fraction of the messages we have received, or the conversations we have had from different ones, but they afford the reader glimpses of character, life, and thought in the spirit world that may not have been brought out in other places.

The first one indicates something of the interest that is aroused on the spirit side concerning the work of communication between the two worlds. Incidentally, the skeptic will have some difficulty, I think,

43

in explaining how or why it originated in the subconscious mind of the psychic, which, of course, is where such critics are inclined to place such writings.

Without any preliminary introduction the following was written:—

"Will you listen to one who wishes to know the sensation of talking to someone on earth again, for he has never communicated since he has been here, and that has been long. He wishes to know if you believe that fear of death can be conquered by means of communication?"

'We feel and believe that many would lose such fear if communication is absolutely proven. Would you not think so?'

"He hears through Mary and answers through her. He does not hear earth sounds yet, for he has had no experience. He is interested now for the first time. I have repeated to him what you said. He says that such conversations must take away the fear of death, because in themselves they are a proof that there is no death.

"He asks what you consider the moral value of such work?"

'We fear that much that comes across does harm; but we believe what is true does enough good to counterbalance. What do you think is the moral value, Mary?'

"First of all, to energize the spirit life on earth; second, to teach that life there is preparing the life here. In short, to vitalize all earth life with spiritual thought and perception."

'Does the visitor hear this?'

"He listens and thinks we may be right; but he is slow to receive new thought."

'Why has he not known of the work of communication?'

"Heaven is immeasurable in space and infinite in its occupations and variety of interests. Not all care to commune with earth; many have never tried, even in all the centuries they may have been here.

"He will ask one more question. Can sinners be saved and sin overcome by the union of the heavenly and earthly influence?"

'We think so; but, Mary, will you not answer that question also?'

"Yes, and always yes, Mary says. But not under the present conditions of mediumship in general. There is too much self in both receiver and sender; there is too much desire for earthly benefits. All this must disappear and the true longing for the heavenly life must appear in both sender and receiver. Then a power could be established which would turn souls away from selfishness and draw the world into the brotherly love we hear so much about."

Along somewhat different lines are several stories that follow. The first came from one who claimed to have known Sis many years ago.

"He is not a teacher, and has not developed all the spirit powers of which he is capable; but he will express to you his own thought as far as he is able."

"I am here, greatly to my surprise. I did not think of death, nor of heaven, nor of the future life, except perhaps in some flash of emotion that passed almost as quickly as it came. And so I am not well prepared to analyze or describe the visions and wonders of this life. But it is a delight to know that the old earth is not entirely lost to us, and that echoes of old familiar voices can be heard across the silence.

"I have not been here very long, and perhaps that is the reason I look a little longingly back to the old home place on earth. Everything here is so far above me, so far advanced, that I feel sometimes that I do not belong here, that I am in a great and wonderful world without

45

proper equipment; in a society of wonderful people, yet feeling myself hopelessly ignorant. Can you guess how that is?

"I have been slow to adapt myself because I had no fitness to begin with. I was not blessed with either a psychic or a poetic or a spiritual nature, just an ordinary man, working along material lines, and never dreaming that I needed any other outfit for this plane except an honest endeavor to live a decent and upright life. And here I am; glad to be accepted, but feeling my ignorance and unworthiness painfully."

Mary added:—

"We have brought this friend to you because we wish you to know what happens to the souls who have never thought of or aspired to anything better; for these are the ones we wish to influence *there.*"

Another communicator expressed his ideas as follows:—

"I am not of any particular name, age, or dramatic experience; yet I feel that all experience here is dramatic and wonderful beyond expression. Mary has tried repeatedly to give you some comprehensive idea of this life, but considers all descriptions thus far as failures so far as definite descriptions go, and she allows me to speak now, wondering if another influence may possibly give another viewpoint.

"Life! What is it? Eternity! Why and how?

"Could you put answers to these questions in words? We fail! Could you succeed? We are out in what is to you the Great Unknown. How shall we put that unknown into words? Time by human reckoning is no more! The present, fair, joyous beyond description. The future, a happy anticipation!

"Terms of feeling, you say? Yes, that is true. For the concrete—the occupations, the activities—we scarcely have language to describe. Remember, when you are asking of our occupations, that you are asking for descriptions of activities, of materials, of joys, unknown to earth.

46

"Activities? Can you conceive of spirit movement faster than light? Materials? The use of substance which in your language is not material, but in ours more solid and enduring than the earth itself? So how can we bring our activities to your conception? Science on earth is peering into the unseen: into electron, atom, ether, energy; yet has scarcely learned the first letter of the alphabet, has scarcely touched the outer rim of our world."

Out of the dozens and even hundreds of experiences contained in our voluminous records I am selecting several more that will be given without further comment, except to say that they came through Sis's pencil; and if after reading them the critic still insists that they are all from her subconscious mind, he must begin to realize that the burden is assuming enormous proportions.

"My name is Julius. We would not be known to you. Many souls are wandering through the heavenly places, and many look back longingly to their old home on earth; for some of us have left there those we loved, and we wish to tell them that *all is well*. We are of those who wish to send good news to earth and tell those we love that *Heaven is Heaven* after all, for we were of a company who scarcely believed in any life beyond the grave, nor did we realize any God in the universe.

"We were 'fed up' on realism and atheistic literature, and our lives were spent without hope of any existence beyond the earthly one. And so we have remained in the unconscious state for a long time—*years*, I think, though one does not measure time here in that way. Now that we have come into the consciousness of life, *real and unending life*, we wish to send the wonderful news to those who like ourselves were groping in darkness.

"Mary is not here, but I do not think she would object to our writing. I am writing for several—I mean I am trying to express the thought of several. I have not been conscious long, but I begin to see the marvels here and the possibilities for the soul."

Here the writing changed and became more emphatic.

"What a mystery! What a wonder! What a joy it all is! We are here trying to express the inexpressible! Can you understand?

"I am another of this group. I am not Julius. I am one who never thought or cared for the future, the future beyond the mortal life; just interested in the occupations and pleasures of the present. What shall I say to help souls there to begin to *think, really think*, along the borders of the Unseen. Mortal mind cannot comprehend *fully* this life, the human brain is not capable; and probably a wise ruler intended that we should live one world at a time. But there is no reason why the human brain should not accept one thought and make it the center of influence in the mortal life. If I could give the thought, it would be something like this:—

'I am living in a mortal world which is the first stage of the human existence. During this stage I am preparing for another one, and that other and farther existence is dependent upon the unseen qualities of my soul, and the education I give to these qualities.'

"This is very crudely expressed, but if only the one thought could sift into the human brain, of the..."

The writing stopped; but soon began again:—

"Mary is here and has met the souls who have been trying to send news to earth. It is well. For they are trying to tell their old friends of the *reality* of this life, that they may come to them without the years of ignorance and delay."

"We wish to give a few words from a stranger who has just called. You know little of the spirits wandering through space. Some of the spirit forms are always near. We are not limited to any sphere; that is, any for which our advancement is sufficient. And all can come to earth; do not forget that. This one was wandering about, and he is one who still loves those who are there, and wishes he might get word to them. Can you take his words?"

'I will try, certainly.'

"Well, here I am then. Here I am, trying to get back to the old earth, when I was so disgusted with it in life that I was ready to leave. I was a businessman, and one of those despised creatures sometimes called politicians. We were a queer lot, and I often cringed inwardly at the selfishness and deceit we all practiced. But one selfish idea led to another, and I guess we were too deep in the mire to pull ourselves out onto firm land, to a firm basis of honesty and unselfishness. I had to come here to realize the depths of trouble and wrongdoing with which we were connected. And yet we passed for pretty respectable men there, and were looked up to as promoters of industry and big business.

"Well, I see clearly now. It is not easy to see clearly there, when manifold interests and many people are concerned in the success of a certain something."

'Is there any special message you wish to send?'

"I wish I *could* say it! I wish I had the power to make my words sink deep, deep into the consciousness of every leader of men, of everyone connected with the money-making business of life! It does not need to be big business either, for the dishonest methods are insidious, and start far down the scale, with pennies and dollars as well as with millions of money.

"Ah, well! The old world will go on, I suppose, sending all sorts to this side. But there is an awakening here, and a poignant sorrow for wasted opportunities.

"That is all. I'll go now. Stranger."

Then Mary added:—

"He did not get his whole message through because words failed him, failed to express his deep feeling and his desire to send a

49

bombshell of truth into the midst of his old political associates. But perhaps you can get his feeling, his unrest, and his desire to do something to make things different."

"We wish you to look back and see who could come to you out of the past. It is a man who lived to be old on earth, but who has renewed his youth here."

After some efforts he was recognized.

"I did not think you would remember!"

Sis replied:—

'No wonder you wanted to come and talk. You did not believe in anything like religion when on earth!'

"No. I had a life without the vision of any hereafter. I was antagonistic to religion and to what I had heard of God. We think strange thoughts over there, with only the human mind and human experience to help. I was moderately happy with my books and my solitude; but by and by sickness came. I went to a hospital and never came out of it into the earth life again. Will you imagine me in a hospital cot, hating the world, the future and the past, and wholly disbelieving in any kind Power above who would or could mitigate my disappointments and trials.

"Everything was dark; and then came total darkness!

"That was years ago, I think. How I passed over, how I came into smothered consciousness, only to lose myself in sleep and unconsciousness again, you may guess. After a long time—years, I guess—a partial sense of freedom came. I could move, could see dimly. I became conscious that I lived! But where? That I could not tell. Through it all, unknown to me, loving guides were telegraphing to my consciousness the lessons which would lead me into the quiet and take away the antagonism.

"It was a long time. But at last I realized that I had left the earth, left my body, lost the old antagonism, and was ready to learn.

"I will skip the rest, and tell you that my spirit powers are developing, and I look forward with increased interest and wonder at the life here. Wonderful! Wonderful!"

A teacher who comes to us frequently had been writing for us one evening and I commented on the character of the writing, saying I suspected its backhand style was much like what she used on earth. She replied:—

"I wrote back-handed, I know, but I do not believe I wrote well. I don't remember that I did anything well; just an attempt to keep soul and body together, and I did not know I had a soul either."

'Do you know how long you have been there?'

"No, we lose out so on time, and I have not thought much about it. I did not count time much in life; it was just many weeks that came and went, and one hard task after another. Oh, the change! Can you wonder that in the bliss of this life, with all that it means to me in every happy moment, that I forget those weary distracting days?"

'Are your parents on that side?'

"Yes, but I do not see them. 'Each to his own place,' as the Bible says. I know that there was no congeniality between us. We tried to do our duty and that was all."

'How old were you?'

"Something over thirty. But the years have all dropped away from me now, and when in some instant of remembrance I see that wrinkled, careworn, ignorant and unhappy woman, I can scarcely believe or realize that it was I. But we must have a happy thought to part with. This is an awful picture that I have looked back upon. What picture shall I present? What but joy! Joy! Fullness of joy and love unspeakable!"

One day when I was away from home, Sis received the following through the pencil:—

"We have something for you, for there is one here who knew you long ago, a former companion, we think; she went to school with you."

The name of Grace Gordon came to her mind, a schoolmate who had passed over when scarcely more than a child.

"We think it is she."

'Did she not tell you her name?'

"Names do not always count here; anyone can assume any name for the time being. We recognize more by the spirit impression. We feel the truth of the recognition much as you describe your sensation: as an electric thrill which assures you of the truth of the communication, or of the person."

'And so, Grace Gordon, you are really here?'

"Yes, I am here, and it is many years since I came over. We were playmates, though I lived rather far away, and I came over here so soon."

'I remember how puzzled we were over your illness.'

"I was frightened when I began to believe I had to die; for who would not be frightened, brought up in the orthodox beliefs as we were? I grew so weak finally that even fear grew feeble, and then unconsciousness. Then an awakening, surrounded apparently by pure white light, with the feeling of wonderful life and strength such as I had not known on earth. Then the experience of a tender surrounding care and loving friendliness. Was it not a joy for a poor frightened child to come into such environment?"

'What have you been doing all these years?'

"Oh, at first just study and recreation, just getting acquainted. Then more study, an acquiring of knowledge with such ease that study became a delight. And so the years have passed; pleasure, study, work for others, and through it all an ever-increasing pleasure. This is life as we know it here."

During a message that was given through my pencil, Sis had expressed some doubts. When she took the pencil, it wrote:—

"There is one here who would like to talk with you. He says:—

"You are right to doubt all things unless they are proved true, but has not this life been proved true to you many times? We know your desire for tests and yet more tests. I will give you one. I am an old acquaintance of yours. Who am I?"

'I do not know. Why is that a test?'

"It will be if you can take my name either by pencil or impression. Stop now and think. You are thinking 'Willis,' but Willis who?"

Sis guessed several names but none seemed to apply.

"You do not get it. We will try later."

I then wrote again for a time, but Sis finally took the pencil and asked:—

'I am wondering if the 'Willis' is not Willis Coleman?'

"Yes."

'Can he talk with me now?'

"Yes."

'Have you been there long?'

"No, I have not been here long, but I found you were writing, and I have always remembered your name."

'Well, I imagine you would be one who would appreciate the beauties there to the full extent?'

"You are right. My highest hopes, my deepest reverence, my desire for happiness, could not have brought me into more perfect conditions."

'Were you unconscious long after arriving there?'

"Not very long, they tell me. I was ill for a time and left the old earth in an unconscious state. It seemed to me I was drifting, drifting slowly into the dark, but not a terrible dark; a time of rest in which I was content. Then into the darkness came a faint light, and the light grew stronger and brighter, and through all my being there ran a thrill of life, life in abundance. Then I awoke to a vision such as I had never dreamed. Beauty, love, all seemed blending in one beneficent power about me, and I felt enveloped and translated into a bliss I had never imagined. Such is heaven."

'You had no sorrow for those left behind?'

"Not then. The glory came first. Then remembrance came, and I wished to look back to the life I had left. They told me of you, and here I am."

'Well, I hope I can talk with you again?'

"I am coming again; Mary says I can. Mary and Dee—your Dee—have charge of this circle. I would like to tell you of their beautiful spirits, but they place a silence on my lips."

Another old friend was brought to Sis at another time. She asked:—

'Is this truly William Andrews?'

"Yes, I am here. I did not know you were writing until a short time ago, and since then I have been waiting to get my chance to say a word. How strange! How very strange it is, because so infinitely different from what we were taught, and in our halfhearted way tried to believe when on earth."

'You find it so different then?'

"Yes, although this is not the highest heaven; we might just say the border of the infinite kingdom. But all is so natural, all so beautiful, and so like our highest dreams, if we had such dreams and desires."

'Yes, I feel myself fortunate to have had even glimpses.'

"You may well be. I had only the old orthodox conceptions, a dim cloudy vision of harps and choirs and a sort of eternal Sunday. Ah! How I wish I could describe it to you! But I think I can only give you the idea of a natural life on earth, but with all pain and sorrow removed, all bickering's, all quarrels, wars, or epidemics or disease—in fact all evil, all discomfort—removed, and only happiness and joyous health, and beauty of surroundings, and then friendships and occupations such as one's heart desires. I feared to come, and regarded the approaching end as a fearful calamity, never knowing that it was the open door to a country so fair that I could have no regret."

'Will you know me when I come?'

"Why not? We cannot fail to recognize our former friends. That is one of the things that belong to spirit perception. It never fails. Well, the old world wraps people up in strange beliefs, and they little know the consequences of their mistaken conclusions."

'Are they always to blame? They reason from certain facts that come before them?'

"Not entirely, but there is a simple law of cause and effect, and it is the working out of that law which may make or break the happiness of a life for a long time. You see such results on earth, do you not?"

'Yes, but I hoped that in heaven such mistakes were overcome?'

"Not all. Mistakes can warp character and life interests and cast their shadow over this fair land."

'This doesn't sound like Mary?'

"No, I am not Mary. Just a stranger who wandered in. I know what mistaken thought and belief can do, for I had worked out a very different theory of the final outcome of the earth life from that which I find here, and I too had to suffer the effect of mistaken judgment. It is all right though,—I mean the law of individual responsibility. And out of our very mistakes and failures we often reap a veritable blessing. You see, human life is one of experiment and growth, failure and success, pain and pleasure, privation and privilege. But all of these qualities are weaving themselves into a strand of experience and wisdom. Don't you see? Character forming even through our mistakes and blundering. Never dwell on the darkened past except to let it lead you into brighter paths."

"I am not Mary; I have just drifted in. I am interested in getting information over to earth people, but have not had much practice. I haven't much to say now, just a greeting from here.

"Can you think what a jolt it would be to some on that side if they really felt this was possible? But they do not believe it. That is the trouble; and they will not advance as long as they continue the narrow lives which at present bind them. Too bad, isn't it? Many of them are doing good, but how much more good they could do if they would only understand! Some do not make very good use of their knowledge, but with most it should startle them into higher thought and wiser action. Most of those who believe that life persists have such a shadowy belief, fanciful instead of practical."

"We are bringing one to you who wishes to talk across the silence. He has not been here long and has not talked with earth people before."

Then this newcomer wrote:—

"Wonder of wonders! Heaven and earth brought together by a power more subtle and more compelling than words! I am the father of a family, but the first to cross to the unseen side. I suppose most people ask first for their families. But I am so sure that all is well with them that I wish first to ask—Well, I guess it is the riddle of the universe; for—Why is life? Why the earthly before the heavenly? Why the ignorance over there? Why, oh why, when spirit from this side can influence souls on that, why the indifference and ignorance there of the one great truth, the continuance of life in the spirit, the continuance of life under new conditions for which we should have prepared over there?"

We asked if he had felt any interest in spiritism when on earth.

"No, not a particle! I thought it an idle study for decadent minds. I was not a church member, but I prided myself on the fact that I loved justice and honesty. Now I see that I had only a fraction of these, for I had a strong color prejudice, thought the white races owned, or should own, the earth. I guess I was honest in dollars and cents, but how could I have been really honest when willing that a nation or a person should take away lands and homes from those who were weaker—Indians, Mexicans, and others of the colored races?"

Sis replied:—

'I think you have answered your own question of *why*. You closed your perceptions to the higher thought of the Fatherhood of God and the Brotherhood of Man.'

"Perhaps you are right; but it seems to me as if there were dynamic force enough here to rule the earth life."

Sis asked:—

'How about freedom of choice?'

"There it is again! Mary has been preaching that to me already."

'Would you prefer to be an automaton, ruled by other will than your own?'

"No! By all that is progressive and interesting, no! I guess you have the right end of the argument!"

THE CHINESE PHILOSOPHER AND RELIGION

"We do not make much of religion as it exists on earth; creed and form are things of no value to us. But we do have at all times a feeling of reverence for, and frequently a desire to worship, the Great Creator. We see so plainly here the moving Power behind all; we see so clearly that the design is planned to make man the culminating figure in the great scheme of things; and we realize so thoroughly the joy and beauty that accompanies man's progress, that we feel we must give thanks for the wondrous things that pertain to it all.

"We do not have churches and congregations; we do not have ministers who pray and preach dogma and doctrine; but we do have great leaders who give much of their time in explaining and counseling concerning the progress of the human soul toward its ultimate goal. This goal we do not know. But we do perceive that it leads us more and more, closer and closer, to the Infinite Power that spreads like a protecting cloak over the entire universe.

"We feel many times that we do not deserve all the blessings that are poured out upon us; we feel so keenly the graciousness of the Great Spirit in allowing us to partake of all the joy and beauty, that

57

we are filled with thankfulness—sometimes almost overpowering us and compelling a prayer of gratitude for it all.

"We have many philosophers who try to expound the mysteries of the future, we have a few mystics whose souls cling to the unutterable things which they believe await them; but with most of us, we are satisfied to move along quietly, filled with a contentment that is never marred.

"You will hardly be able to fully understand it until you come. In the busy material life the soul usually fails to comprehend the grandeur of the Creator's great plan. You may at times think you have glimpses of this plan, but they are reflections only; the full light never reaches you. It is something to feel that there is a Creator; it is a pleasure to imagine there is a plan; but the full significance awaits your arrival on the spirit plane."

Then our leader added:—

"Mary says she has wanted to give something like that several times, but never seemed to be able to put it in words. We do pray here, we do worship, we do feel thankful for the many wonderful things which fill our life. But it is so unlike the churches there with their form and ceremony, that we hardly think of calling it religion; yet it is the very heart and soul of religious experience."

THINKING

We were told that the following message, which came through my pencil, was from Prof. Wm. James. Critics may claim that it does not sound like his phraseology. They are ever ready to do that. But it should be noted, even by them, that it is quite different in style from many other communications in the book. And such critics should also bear in mind that we have been told many times of the difficulties surrounding the work of communicating: that the idea

58

is impressed on the mind of the medium, but that the phraseology often takes on characteristics of the medium's own writing.

"When we use the brain to send out a new thought we are performing an act that is as mysterious as life itself. No one knows how it is done. The process has been studied here for ages, and it is no nearer a solution. We believe that those on higher planes have arrived at some sort of explanation; but life and thought on higher planes take on an ethereal quality that we fail to comprehend.

"We know that the process of thinking is governed by what we term will. But this only complicates the problem. For we know no more of the working of will power than of the formation of thought. They go together, that is all.

"When one tries to fathom some of these mysteries one realizes that the Creator was wise in making mysteries. Nothing stimulates endeavor more than an unsolved problem or an unexplained mystery.

"When we are willing to admit that there are no more mysteries, we must acknowledge that we have learned everything there is to know. And what would existence be worth then? To know is a satisfaction; but to know all would be stagnation. We believe that there will always be mysteries ahead of us to lure us on. We cannot conceive of advance without them. But when we are able to fathom some mysterious depth we experience a sense of achievement that makes one of the joys of our existence. You will never feel a greater thrill than when you learn the answer to the question, 'What is life?' But when will you experience that thrill? Not on this plane; not on immediate planes. Perhaps it is the greatest and final mystery. Perhaps when we solve that we will have reached our ultimate goal!

"It is interesting to speculate on these questions. It is satisfying to feel that we are at least attempting to understand some of the problems before us. But when we stop and inquire what else we would have to live for if these were all known, we feel the future would be blank and uninteresting.

"When you find that life consists of problems to solve, you find some meaning in the evils and obstacles of the earth existence. No one could achieve much who met nothing to conquer. No one would find life interesting if he encountered no problems. We grow by striving. We enjoy by conquering.

"When life grows too distressing because of the problems and obstacles, there is always the knowledge that the greatest hindrances are soon to be passed, and that the future is one where we only strive as we feel the urge. In this future no necessity demands our labor when the spirit falters. We have no more stimulating thought than the knowledge that we can make our greatest struggles when life is just beginning; that after the first difficulties—the difficulties of the earth life—are overcome, we can choose the time to try to solve other problems, to undertake other tasks.

"When life on earth is over, the greatest joy comes from feeling that one has mastered the difficulties it held in a masterful way; that is, that one has succeeded in accomplishing satisfactorily all the tasks that have been placed before him.

"You may never know the supremest joy of overcoming all difficulties until you arrive at life's goal in the infinite future. But you will experience succeeding joys that make existence worth while."

After the above was written I turned the pencil over to Sis, and Mary added:—

"We also wish to give you something about our own familiar life here. We are not always probing mysteries, Wm. James to the contrary."

'Is he still there?'

"No, but we will confess to him when he comes!

"We have our home life—a real home life of pleasant intercourse and occupation. We have our studies, which of course do include some of the mysteries. And we have travel and entertainment in a thousand ways. Wm. James forgot for the moment his own love of music, drama, travel, intercourse with friends, and—"

"All these go to the making of our happiness here."

'Well, I am glad you have told us that we do not have to have 'highbrow' mysteries all the time!'

"We would be shut out if you did. This is Dee. You remember my despair when things got too deep for me?"

'Yes. It is a little easier for you now, is it not?'

"Yes, I have a better comprehension. But I do not have to go very far before reaching my limit, even now!"

GHOSTS

"Ghosts are the uneasy spirits who have left some earth duty undone or some wrong unrighted, and they try to go back again. The spirit of one who has committed a crime, or who has wronged someone on earth, is never at rest until the wrong is made right. Let this be a lesson to evildoers. There are uneasy souls here who never have peace because they cannot undo the wrong. Criminals learn the lesson too late, and if reincarnation were true they would gladly go into another earth life to profit by the lesson they have learned here. We wish we could make this plain to all evildoers."

Do you say they *never* have peace? Do you mean that literally?'

"We mean it in connection with mortal life. Of course the one who has suffered comes here sooner or later, and then the opportunity arrives for righting the wrong.

"We have many here who are making a study of these wandering spirits, and it is found that they sometimes seem to be seeking lost treasure which to them is of transcendent importance."

We had occasion to speak of some ghostly manifestations which were recorded in the newspapers.

"There are certain dark phases of spirit life, and there are spirits who do not leave their malicious propensities on earth. We teach and control them whenever possible, and lead them into higher life. There are no prisons here for evil ones. There are no chains to bind them or hinder their progress. All we can do is to control through thought influence. But such natures do not easily receive impressions for good. The evil ones on earth cannot always be reached by pure and kindly teaching either. Those who are hardened in sin are long in changing."

'There seem to be more ghosts in Europe than here. Why is this?'

"The old castles and houses have remained through many generations; have survived since the days of war, cruelty, and oppression. They have given rise to many uneasy spirits, some working out their own evil propensities, and some trying to rise above their former state. America is newer; yet here are many who have committed crimes, and it is not impossible for them to appear. But you need not fear any interference."

'Do you see many of the murderers and criminals there?'

"No, we are not their guides; that work belongs to the missionary circles here. They try with unceasing efforts to bring them into an unselfish life. But the results are oftentimes slow and hard to see."

'There is still plenty of crime here.'

"That is the result of long waywardness and evasion of authority. Such things do not happen suddenly. The preparation of this wave of crime has been going on for a long time."

Something brought up the subject at another time, and we asked Mary to explain further.

"I can only repeat that the spirits of criminals often return and live over again the atrocities for which they are still suffering. It is the law of cause and effect. Their subconscious selves received the impressions of their acts and beliefs so strongly that they are still bound by the old sensations and criminal instincts, and they try to reproduce the semblance of the crimes or incidents that caused these impressions, in the surroundings in which they occurred. They live it over again as an actor reproduces a scene he has memorized. It is through the terribleness of these scenes that they discover themselves for what they are. It is sometimes a lifetime before they turn away from their evil impulses. But it is this earth-walking, this renewing of their past crimes in memory, that finally makes them determine to try for something better."

INFANTS IN SPIRIT LAND

In the appendix to the previous book, *Spirit World and Spirit Life*, will be found considerable information as to how the little ones are met and cared for. In the following section is an account of our communications with two who went over as infants many years ago.

"They are not pure spirits yet," we are told, "for then they would belong to the angelic host. They came as infants, but they possessed the immortal spirit, and they differ only in the fact that they have never known sin nor earthly life—material life, I should say."

'What do you have that they do not?'

"We have the knowledge of good and evil, and the power of choice, and the education through this to help others who are still in the world of good and evil. But there are many other ways in which they can serve."

These infant spirits are infants no longer, for they have been there an ordinary lifetime. They wrote one evening:—

"We think it is interesting to watch these messages to and fro. Can you give us a thought from earth now?"

I don't know that this should have surprised us, but it did. We all at once realized that they knew nothing of earth or material things by experience, anymore than we knew spirit life by experience. Sis asked if they could not see material things:—

"They are untrained in that respect. What they would like to know is how you manage to live with all those earthly impediments they hear about?"

I asked if they had ever been brought in contact with evil on that side.

"Not very much. They could not become teachers, for they have no earthly experience. Their work is along other lines. They are trying hard to understand earth life, but many of its phases seem almost unbelievable to them. The crime and cruelty they only know by descriptions, but they look at it as an almost unbelievable fiction. They do not fully realize it anymore than you fully realize this life. They have been taught and believe it as you believe some faraway facts of ancient history. Perhaps that is not a good comparison either, for you have at least some other earthly happenings to compare it with. But they have not, so it is hard for them to understand."

They were much interested, as they said, and came often to the circle. Many months later we were talking with them again and the following was written:—

"We are learning the earth language, and often listen to the conversations between you and the circle. It seems very wonderful to us—very wonderful that people on earth are willing to live in the midst of such sin, misery, sickness, ignorance, and poverty, and all the other ills we hear you describe."

'Do you not see the ignorant and criminal ones who come over there?'

"We are not really in touch with them, for we do not try to influence the earthborn mortals when they first come over. Our work with them is afterward in trying to help them to the various occupations here."

'You seem to come together; are you together all the time?'

Mary says: "They came over so young that they received most of their education together, and they grew into a companionship that has become a habit as well as a joy. They are alike in temperament, so that naturally they grew into intimate companionship."

I asked if such infants reached maturity earlier there than here.

"Yes, because they learn more rapidly. One of them came over several years before the other. He was far more mature than if he had remained on earth for that time. He met his little brother and was his helper for a long time, and his father taught him to love the family tie wherever congeniality existed. Then they took up studies together because both were interested in the same things."

'Having no sin or selfishness to overcome, I should have thought they would be on a higher plane by this time?'

"They could go at any time, and they are connected with circles who are studying higher things. But their father preferred to remain near the earth-plane, and they have loved him and stayed with him."

'How does the earth appear to them?'

Mary says: "They look upon it as a mystery and—"

"Will you listen to them?"

"We are not able to comprehend many things. We hear of the mechanical devices there and wonder much about them. We move in a flash of time. You are studying ways of getting about upon the surface of the earth, in the air, on the water, or maybe under the water. We have heard of your submarines and airplanes, automobiles and railroad trains. It all seems so slow, so difficult, so unnecessary! How do you ever find time to move from one place to another! Then

65

you have to spend so much time in sleep. And Mary tells us that you have to spend time and strength and money in providing things to eat and drink. How can you be patient with it all?"

'Have you studied the earth enough to be able to sense or understand material things as compared with your spiritual objects?'

The reply seems to us to show that they do not fully understand, for they still refer to actions rather than to things.

"We try to understand. We try to move as slowly as your fastest travel, and we grow impatient. We can have some sensation of taste, but we cannot understand how people would ever be willing to spend much time at it. We have tried our best to sleep, but we could not succeed, and can only guess how that is accomplished. You see we are handicapped when we try to help earthborn persons when they first arrive here."

Much later, we were talking again and asked Mary about them.

"They are here, and are talking among themselves about earth affairs. They are as much interested about the earth as you are to hear about us."

'Have they just become interested since we began to write?'

"They did not know much about it before that. They were not drawn to it in any way, and simply lived the spirit life as it manifested itself here."

'What are they interested in? What do they wish to know?'

"About the daily life, the work and the pleasures, and the conditions generally."

'I do not suppose they understand how it seems to get tired, so weary that it seems almost impossible to move?'

"Not at all. They do not know the sensations of weariness. They want you to tell them how it feels?"

Sis tried to picture such a condition.

66

"That, they think, must spoil life entirely!"

Then they themselves asked:—

"How do you get over it?"

Sis described how rest was taken.

"Well, what next?"
'We also recuperate our powers by eating. That you do not know much about?'
"No, not from necessity. We have tasted fruit here and think it good, only we forget to eat it as a rule."
'You do not know hunger then?'
"No. How does it feel?"

After that was described, they remarked:—

"What a bother! We are glad we do not live there. How do you get about?"
'I suppose you do not know much about our methods of travel?'
"No, only as you have told us."
'Do you have horses there?'
"Not that we have seen. I have heard about them."

We then tried to tell them the speed of the trains, saying that it was about a mile a minute. But as they knew nothing of either a mile or a minute, that did not mean anything to them. We then said that perhaps they had some idea of the length of a day because that was the time between one time of our writing and the next.

"That tells us a little. But we do lots of things between times. And we can travel, oh, so far! How far would it be in miles?"

MISCELLANEOUS ADVICE

"Try to do your own work, your own little task, without fear and without doubt of yourself. Just use your psychic power as we give it to you, and then trust the Great Power behind and above us all, whose will does accomplish miracles upon earth, and can bring peace and happiness and spiritual knowledge to those who keep the open mind.

"You fear your own mind is writing this. I tell you it is not, but is being impressed from here, from across the border, from the beautiful world beyond the tumult and discord of earthly strife. How can the world get a new revelation unless through the minds or souls that are in tune with the heavenly vibrations? Be at peace. Your work is not your own; it is guided from here.

"We cross the border to you. Do you realize how narrow that border is, and how near it lies to heavenly happiness?

"The messages that have come over to you will be a perpetual blessing to the many who will read and believe. It was not intended that all mortals should see through the gateway into the other world. It is not in accordance with the decision of personal free will, personal responsibility and choice. Yet in these latter days the spiritual revelation is more and more coming to the world, and it remains for the world to accept or reject, even as it was left to those of Christ's time to accept his teachings or reject them. And the influence of His teachings, although accepted by such a pitiful few at that time, has been the great saving power of humanity."

'If you could tell me the greatest duty of this life, what would you say?'

"That is a rather difficult question to answer. But you may drop all the church creeds, for church creeds have been in the way of pure religion. *To serve, to help others, to think kindly and act generously and wisely*—these are the earth part of your service. The rest will come to you as you move toward the light of our perfect spiritual life. Moving always: that is a great, but sometimes a solemn truth. For movement might be in the wrong direction. Service, dear friend. Do not think we are constantly thinking only of the acquirement of knowledge. Development without service is apt to lead to selfishness."

"We have a message from one here who has waited some time for a chance to write. He is a man who has been on this side for a long time, but has had little desire to write. But of late he has felt that perhaps he could give something that might be worthwhile. He says:—

"I am not accustomed to expressing my thought, but I would like to try to tell the earth people that they are straying from the path which leads to happiness here. It is with much sorrow that we see the tendency to turn away from spiritual ideals and seek only the transient and trivial things which amuse. We wish that the idea that they are laying the foundations of their future life now could be impressed upon them. In some way they should be made to understand that the things of the spirit are the only lasting things. All amusement, all frivolity, vanish at the touch of the death angel. And with most of the members of the human race there is so little left. (While writing this I felt that the complaint against amusement was mostly that it was not lasting; not that it was sinful unless it excluded all else; or that there was no amusement in the spirit world.) We mourn over it as we see how little effect our influence has on many. We wish that in some way we could overcome this wrong tendency, and instill a little understanding of the vital things of life.

"Tell the Christians there to serve others by assuring them of the life here; but also that this life depends for its happiness on their own spirit preparation while there. We cannot make the fact too strong that human belief and human activity prepare each mortal for his life here. If the belief and the activity are in the wrong direction, years may pass before they see clearly the true spirit life, and come into their own spirit powers. I was one who made the mistake of too much creed, too much of what is called fundamentalism. It overshadowed the love of Christ in my soul, and I wandered in darkness for a long time."

RIGHT LIVING

"We would like to have you write for a visitor. He is interested in the welfare of those who are continually arriving to begin their life on this side. We will let him write."

"I am desiring to place before the world some information that seems to me of much importance. I am a lover of humanity, and a sort of caretaker of souls who come to this side. I have studied for many years the various attitudes with which these newcomers view the change. I find almost as many differences as there are different personalities. But I feel that I have learned to divide them roughly into three classes.

"First and fewest are those who have looked forward with pleasure and understanding to a future life, believing it but a glorious continuation of the earthly existence.

"Second are those whose number is very large, who have led lives of helpfulness on earth, who may or may not have believed in a future life, but who were ready to adopt new ideas whenever they felt that they were good.

"Then there is the third class, to which it seems to me a very large majority must be assigned. These are never able to understand the new life until after long and sometimes painful periods have passed.

"Now why is that so? Why should such a vast number be condemned to a slow and difficult progress? They are not all evil; not even a very large number are conspicuously evil. But they have somehow failed to obtain the proper education that fits one for entrance into this life. We have to care for them, nurse them, and educate them. It is a blessed work for many of us, but such an unnecessary one. I

70

wish I could present my ideas more forcibly, for I feel that the earth people should be made to realize these conditions.

"When Christ came to earth it was for the express purpose of explaining these very things. But his following seem to have woefully failed to understand his teachings. I think nothing would be of more benefit to the world than an understanding of the value of helpful, loving service. And when one learns that such a life is the one best fitted to progress here, then the knowledge is doubly valuable. We are striving in every way to get this knowledge before the world."

THE EARTH ONLY A SCHOOL

"We are not your usual friends. Do you wish us to write?"

'Certainly, if you have something good to tell us.'

"We will try to tell you of our work today. Not today as you know it, but for a 'time' as we know it.

"We will introduce ourselves first. We are two who have learned much from your true guides, Mary and Dee. And we are now studying in other circles for power and more power, that we may send messages to earth that will attract the attention of the careless and give inspiration and comfort to the thoughtful.

"If you could realize the need as we do, we believe you would make it your life's work, and let nothing interfere with our messages."

'What do you see of the need for them, more than we see?'

"We see that so-called religion has failed to convert the world. Many saint-like souls are within the church, but the great multitudes outside are an opposing influence."

'Many outside are also pure and wise.'

"Yes, we know this, and we depend upon them. But how to reach the thoughtless, the criminal, or the foolish ones of earth is the serious question here. Each must help, we here and you there."

'How can you best help here?'

"Make your thoughts known; try for influence; tell others of our presence."

'But when we do they do not believe.'

"Use your influence and do not be discouraged if the results are not as great as you wish. Each can do something. Only the kindness taught by loving spirits, only the wisdom which can make kindness a living power, only the constant reiteration of the fact that life on earth is only a school, and only the beginning of the spirit education; only the truth, the almost tragic truth, that the soul arrives here just as it left the earth—no better, no wiser—and that true happiness here is in their own power, and must come from their own adaptation to the laws of spirit life. These things must be the foundations of the teachings from here. Mary and Dee are doing much good, but they must depend on mortal power and influence after all."

'Can you tell us who you are?'

"We are two who loved each other on earth, and found each other here after the change that you call death. There is no death, be sure of that. But happiness must come from one's own nature, one's own receptivity to spirit knowledge, one's own lovingness and desire to help others."

PERSONALITY

"We have many teachers on this side. They are all fine characters, but mostly very different in personality. We value each for himself.

"We make more of individual personality than you do. Unless uselessly eccentric, it is considered a valuable asset to be more or less different from others. We recognize the value of variety, and cultivate all characteristics that bring it about. We do not like to be just like someone else in anything except the desire to acquire knowledge. In the use of that knowledge we develop our individuality. We have those, of course, who carry it to excess, just as you have there. But ordinarily it is someone who has not fully developed the other sides of his personality, and his eccentricity is overlooked as far as possible."

'Do all of these varieties of personality desire to study?'

"Yes, to a certain extent. The kind of knowledge one seeks shows the trend of character, and the use of the knowledge acquired develops it.

"Personality is the greatest fact in the universe. We here believe so thoroughly that man is the final achievement in the universal plan, that we recognize at once that the most perfect man would be the highest achievement. And the most perfect man is the one who best succeeds in filling his appointed niche; which means the one who makes the best use of the talents he possesses. If all were given the same talents all would achieve the same perfection if they were successful; and we know that such a condition would not be satisfactory. But where there are different perfections, different personalities, we have a variety that is endlessly satisfying."

SPIRIT INFLUENCE ON EARTH LIFE

"I am trying to imagine what is needed on earth, and then I try to put my influence in the scale to bring that gift to humanity. Not much, you may say, but here the human life looks such a blind unthinking thing, that we want to give it a forward inspiration. It is a thousand pities that the great gift of knowledge of this life should so often have to come through the offices of selfish mediums who may be inclined to financial speculations. Such persons do not really sense the heavenly gift; they get only some small unworthy conceptions which they repeat to credulous humans for the shekels it may bring.

"We here grieve over this condition, but are earnestly trying to send a true word through mediums who wait in patience and faith for illumination. Do your bit, as the soldiers said, and let the world have the truth to accept or reject as it will. The truth is coming to earth. Be glad to help in its introduction. For it is coming more and more through influential minds which cannot be charged with foolishness or insanity or commercialism."

"You must remember that we are always trying to help the earth people in their progress. We usually keep this in mind in all our work, and if we feel that we have something especially valuable for them, we try to impress someone with the idea. In doing this we are accustomed to work in large groups; we do not ordinarily work alone as we did on earth. When something new is discovered or thought of, it is usually common property—the combined thought of a large number. Then we try to influence as many as we conveniently can to work with us in sending this new thought earthward."

'Is this done by concentration?'

"Yes, that is the way. We have stated times for this, sometimes large gatherings in one place. We have been aware many times that this influence was felt on earth, and we believe that much of the progress there is caused in this way."

'Do superstitions of savage races come from spirit impression?'

"Possibly. But more often superstition is a growth from some early impression which has not been turned in the right direction. When a people have no spiritual thought it is difficult to impress them with a spiritual idea."

'Can criminals be impressed?'

"We wish they could, but alas, they are the most difficult to impress with ideas that would be uplifting. Their own impulses may receive added strength from malicious influences here.

"We feel that a general good effect results from our efforts, so we consider that we are repaid. Out of the great number on earth, we know there are some who will feel our influence. So we send a general impression and trust to its being picked up there by those who are sensitive. Then we wait for these to spread the influence among others. It is slow work; but evolution has always been slow.

"We wish the truth might be spread more rapidly. But we have to fall back upon the belief that we are only asked or expected to use our little influence in the cause of the great truth."

'Do you think the knowledge of real spiritual truth is spreading?'

"We are told that it is. There is ever a benumbing influence because of money-making mediums who use their powers only as a fortune-telling scheme. But there are more and more educated and spiritual-minded people who believe in the immortality of the soul, and in the truth of the love and life and progress that are made known here."

THE LIFE ON EARTH

"We wish to give you a few words for your comfort. We know how doubtful you are at times, and we can scarcely wonder at it, for we remember our own manner of thought. Yet we did not have the proof of this life that you have had. You did not get much help from church creeds, but strange to say, we did, and had implicit confidence in them. But now we see how man-made many of them were. You need not follow the creeds, as indeed you know yourself. The example of Christ's life is to us the perfection of religious teaching. And one following it is safe, safe from any harm of doctrine."

'I suppose your thoughts do not dwell much on this life?'

"No, except that it is the birthplace of the individual soul. In this respect it becomes of wonderful importance. But the physical part of it has little enough to do with spirit."

'But the physical was all created by spirit, was it not?'

"Yes, I suppose so. The Great Creator used material surroundings for the birth of humanity. We can get no further than this. There is so much—oh, so much—beyond us that we dare not venture on many positive statements. The one thing that seems to us positive is the evolution of humanity. Upward, always upward. Why it started so low down in the earth, we do not comprehend. But the forward look is fair and enticing beyond expression. This is what makes our life here so fascinating."

MAKING US UNDERSTAND

"I have much to tell you if I only knew how to make you understand. We have many wonders that will have to wait until you come. You no doubt think we have told you so much of this life, there is little more to tell. But it will not take you long when you come to see that we have given you only an outline. It is not the material surroundings, as you might call them, that I mean so much as the mental life that opens out before one. It is a strange condition, if you will stop and think, to be where you have what might be called a mental existence only. It is by the mind that everything is done. And to do all that concerns life by just using the mind is a new sensation, and to most people, a new idea. We make ourselves just what our minds are capable of desiring that we should be."

THE REALITY OF SPIRIT LAND

"We are not Mary or Dee; just spirits passing by who caught your call from earth."

'Are you in spirit land?'
"Yes, in our spirit *home*-land."
'Have you land?'
"Not as you perceive land. It is difficult to make the mortal mind comprehend the solidity and permanence of unseen forces and unseen materials. We have homes and meeting places, but all formed from the invisible material—invisible, we mean, to mortal eyes.

"Cultivate your spirit impressions. Know that heaven is truly here, whether visible or not to mortal eyes.

"You there live by unseen forces. Your body could never serve you but for the unseen force of life. Eyes, ears, limbs, even thought, all play upon the wonderful instrument you call body. Do not forget that this mechanism of the body may be as perfect after that which you call death as during life; though all that fine mechanism is without power, because the unseen force called life has withdrawn itself. But it goes on functioning in a new body, and with far greater ease and power than before.

"Try for perfect faith and belief. We are here, truly. Heaven is here, surely."

TWO VISITORS

I had been reading an account of the work of an English medium. As I concluded, Sis took up the pencil and it wrote:—

"We have been watching while he read. We could see his aura perfectly, and by its changing color and expression we could read his mind."

I asked who was writing.

"Not Mary or Dee, but one on this side who is interested in spiritistic development over there. The world needs it; and we here who love the world and believe in its progress, and hope for its final spiritualization, are trying to help by our influence the trend of pure spiritualism. We are grieved as you are at the narrowness, the earthliness, of many who have some of the heaven-given psychic power. But nevertheless we believe in the final progress and influence of pure spiritualism; the honest effort to come into touch with heavenly power, heavenly purity, and heavenly kindness. We go now.

"We are here and know you have had some visitors, and we are glad."

'Who is writing now?'

"We are Mary and Dee. We have been waiting for you, and while we waited two forms appeared, strangers to us, but of wonderful purity and power, we thought. So we watched while they influenced your pencil and transferred their thought to paper.

"We are glad to know of the work being done there in the cause of true communication. When heaven bends to earth to bring to it a blessing, there should be recognition of the gift by those who receive."

THE BAND OF WORKERS

Our leader, Mary, wrote through Sis's pencil:—

"It seems that the world is very unready for spirit influence. But it cannot be worse than it was in times past. All will come right at last. We must hold fast to faith and hope, and do our part as we can."

Here the pencil was seized firmly, trailing off at first in a heavy mark, then dashed forward in bold writing:—

"We are here. We are a band of workers and wish to add our knowledge. We wait not only in hope, but in certainty; for we go far and near and see all sides of the work among many people and many nationalities. There is a slow dawning of a great day. It is coming, coming surely; and we can watch it from afar.

"We were passing and caught the last sentence, and caught your somewhat discouraged attitude. We move quickly, and we wrote quickly. We are a large band, but divide our numbers many times and go to different places. We wish you to feel the spirit presence as you just now felt ours. You have many helpers about you, but you do not always keep your spirit perceptions alert. Can you not keep in constant touch with your spirit friends?"

'How can we do it, with all the material things here to interfere?'

"We do not know. We know we did not. But it would be an ideal condition."

WORKING THROUGH DIVINE INFLUENCE

"We wish to have you take a message from one who feels that all work from this side is important to life on that side."

'Do you mean the communicating is important, or are you referring to the spiritualizing influence?'

"Both. We are exerting much thought force upon mortals, and we grow into stronger power ourselves by trying to help others."

'There is criticism here, saying that spiritualism tends to take God out of religion?"

"We know that is not true. Our very power comes from God, and manifests through His divine effort.'

'The spiritualistic cause also suffers because ignorant and scheming people try to make money out of it.'

"I was not speaking of ignorant or unspiritual ones. I mean only those who look to the higher life, to spirits on higher planes for guidance. All here who in their circles are working for the good of others are really helping the Divine work. And we believe we are given this work to do by the Divine Power whom you call God.

"Never fear. We are impressed to try for the conversion of human thought into spiritual ideals, to impress the thought of unselfish service upon the worldly, to put a check upon mortal or worldly and selfish desires and plans, and to help to bring that 'peace on earth' which has been the desire of all pure spirits for many centuries."

THE MINISTER

"We would like to have you take a message from one here who has not known you nor our work. We will write for him. We wish to prove to him the truth of communication with mortals."

After a short wait this stranger wrote:—

"I am told I can communicate with earth people. I have not believed it possible, nor thought it essential. Yet I can see that it might comfort many. But what else, what other good could it accomplish?"

'We here think that such communication will convince the unbelieving that there is a future life, and also that each and everyone is preparing his own future right now.'

Mary, our leader, wrote:—

'That is why we try so hard to send our words across.'

Then the new communicator went on:—

"Well, I was a minister, and preached the gospel to many. And I was many times confronted with the old question, 'How do you know it is so?' If you can get reliable truth from here, it must have great effect on mortals there."

"Were you a 'revivalist'?"

"Yes, I was one—of a sort. I did preach to the poor and to the socially unknown. The slums of any great city were my church; the love of Christ and the forgiveness of sin, my topic."

'That ought to have saved many.'

"Yes; but as I watched the effect of my work, I saw so many turning back to their sins after the first excitement was over. Mary's way may be the better way (referring to our leader). For the life one lives is after all the final test of character. And in a pure life the love of Christ would be a baptism of love falling upon the soul. Life and character are God's way of bringing human souls into eternal life. And the love of Christ is, after all, the underlying power to save."

Mary took the pencil again and wrote:—

"Mary says, the love of Christ is still the power to save. And for the perfected ones who live near the Most High, we believe it to be preeminent. Tell the world of His life. The trouble with most evangelists is in their teaching of the doctrine of Christ's atonement for all, when it is the character of each that must be weighed in the balance. But some are pure and unselfish and good who never heard of Christ. Do not think that a good life may be considered as naught, if not built exactly on orthodox or fundamental foundations. Many are the 'Children of God' without being especially aware of it. Many are influenced from here who never heard the name of Christ. Do not think for a moment that such are not received. Remember Christ's own words, 'Blessed are the merciful, for they shall obtain mercy. Blessed are the pure in heart, for they shall see God.'

"We believe in the Christ, in his mission to earth. We look to Him for guidance and inspiration. But we do not worship Him in the same way he is worshiped on earth. He wishes his example of peace and loving service to be followed, and it is our joy to follow his example here. But he is not afar off on some throne of glory. He is more like an elder brother, more like a bright and shining example for us to follow."

'Do not some place Christ as one with God?'

"Yes, we have many such, and they are confused and disappointed at first. But they finally come into the true appreciation of the purity and loveliness of his life and character, and are contented and happy."

'I wonder if Christ would approve of all the Easter worship of him?'

"No, we think not. To follow his example, to make each one's own life a blessing to others—this is the religion he tried to establish, and which he hopes will at last become the religion of the world."

'It makes religion a logical and blessed thing to have.'

"We grieve that the world is so far away from the pure and happy belief that should be accepted. The time is coming, and coming fast, when there will be a reconstruction of the religion of the churches. Creeds will largely go, and love and service take their place."

EVIDENTIAL MESSAGES

"If the world wants evidential messages all the time, when do they expect to be convinced? If ten or twenty messages are considered to be perfect evidence, how can ten or twenty more be any better evidence? We think part of this desire for evidence is simply a curiosity to see what new method will be adopted. Most of the skeptics pay no attention to *what the evidence means.* They simply decide whether or not it can be classed as evidence, and then pass it by. If anyone really desires evidence just to decide him in his next step towards accepting all that such a truth implies, he will be satisfied with what evidence has been given. But, alas, too many really do not desire that the truth shall be proven. It is only too apparent that many should change their mode of life, their manner of thinking, if they accept the truth. It is the same thing to many people as being converted to the ideas that the church puts forth. Many turn away because they do not desire the kind of a life that religion and the church teach as the one that should be followed. If they believed that death was the entrance into a life where only the unselfish and the pure of heart could find happiness, they would of necessity change their mode of living."

82

THE DESIRE TO HELP

"How we wish we could see our friends over there. Will the world ever come into the truth, that visible and invisible mingle together, and both are everywhere present?"

'Only a few believe it.'

"Yes, we know; and the hope of the future rests with those few."

'But the bad spirits influence the earth life also?'

"Yes, we know that too. And therein lies the greater need of knowledge. Malicious spirits are ever trying to control human influence. They do succeed many, many times, and selfishness, war, deception, suicides, murders, and a host of other evils are the result. If the world, the human world, only knew, they could then control these influences. But instead of practical work and preventive policies, they punish the wicked when some especially flagrant act brings them to view. We would even leave our blessed happiness here if we could return for a while to give humanity the truth as we have learned it here."

JOAN OF ARC

We had been reading aloud from an account of the life of Joan of Arc written from a psychic viewpoint. Afterwards comments were made through the pencil as follows:—

"We were listening to the reading. We know much of her here. She has advanced to much higher spheres, but her history and accounts of her life here on this plane are in our libraries and are much read. She had a wonderful character to begin with. Then she was influenced by strong spirits here who were working for the nation they still loved. It was during a time when fighting was considered the noblest profession; and the world was in such condition that armies were needed to control the people. We do not think any leader could receive such power now to lead armies. But we do think that leaders for a great movement towards guiding the world into righteous thought could and would be influenced from here, and might even be led as Joan was led.

"It is the thought of some here that such a leader will appear on earth soon. But it is something we know little about. Whether they are saying this with true prophetic power, or whether it is simply a hope that combined influence from here will bring this about, we do not know. When we see the tendencies of much of humanity today we realize that something of this kind should come to pass. We are lending our small influence in that direction, but we are not in the counsels of the great leaders here. You may be sure that influence from here will not be lacking. What effect it will have the future will tell."

SIGHT

"You have taken our last message correctly, as we can see by reading what you have written."

'So you have acquired that ability?'

"Yes, I think I can read as fast as you can write. It is rather a new accomplishment on this side. That is, it is new in this application. We think in this way we can avoid mistakes, and can stop you when you allow wrong words or phrases to come from your subconscious mind."

'Do you actually see the writing, or do you get it in some other way?'

"We do see the writing, but not just as you see it. I fear I cannot describe the process so you can understand it. We do not get it through your mind, but neither do we get it through rays of light coming from the paper."

'Does it make a difference if my writing is less legible?'

"Yes, it does make a difference."

'Then of course you do get it from the writing itself.'

"Yes, but not in the way with which you are familiar."

THE WATCHERS

'Is anyone here?'

"Yes, we are left as watchers, and have waited for you to come."

'Where are the rest of the circle?'

"With friends, exploring some of the planes and circles where spirits dwell."

'Can they go to other planes?'

"Many circles are near, but also Mary and Dee could progress to higher planes if they so desired. But their love for those on earth keeps them here where they can be in touch with you.

"Spirit has powers you can scarcely discern. We are just the watchers while the others are away. But we wish we could give you some knowledge, some realization of the life of the spirit. Many worldly ones feel a keen disappointment when they first arrive, because all is so different, because all depends upon spirit knowledge, spirit powers, which they so entirely neglected to develop when on earth."

THE VALUE OF COMMUNICATION

We remarked that the knowledge that communication was possible should convince people of the truth of a future life, and of the need of right living while here.

"We believe that to be the greatest of all reasons for the coming together of the two worlds. The fact that life goes on without any miracle; that the human soul begins here as it left off there; that there is no wonderful transformation of character; that evil remains evil until the soul turns of its own accord toward the good; that sin does reap its own reward; that there is no hell except the one created by one's own self; that all, all, can rise through gloom, disappointment, sin and selfishness, to something high, holy and grand, and forever and forever live in happiness and usefulness: Are these things worth the thought of mortals?

"That is what we believe, and why we try to send the truths of this life to earth. The world needs a new inspiration. Is that inspiration here and now?"

"It is difficult to impress the world because of the stigma attached to spiritualism,"

'Has the world ever received a great truth at once?'

"The world has come through a great darkness and ignorance. We here who began our conscious life on that planet love it and wish to purify its thought, that mortals who still remain may rise to higher level, and heavenly love and kindness be the law of life. *Think what that would mean!*"

DEATH

We referred to a sentence which had been written some time before, something like this:—

"Death to you is a darkened way; to us it is a path of light."

In reply the pencil wrote:—

"We do not remember it, but it is true. There is no darkness for us as we watch our loved ones coming across the little dividing line. We think that the close of life should be lifted out of its sorrow and fear and regarded only as a peaceful sleep, with a blessed and bright awakening. This of course refers to those who have cultivated their spirit life when on earth. Death may indeed be a darkened path for those who have no fitness for this life;—and yet it is not the death, but the awakening which is so dreary and oftentimes terrible for those whose lives have not been just or merciful or spiritual."

And at another time:—

"One thought we will leave with you. Take no thought nor anxiety for the future life. Have no dread of death, which is only a coming, a rebirth, into this life. Do what you can to help others into an understanding of the immortal life of the human soul, and live in happy contentment and confidence of your future, now and ever."

And still further:—

"Never be afraid of death. It is only the final sleep of the mortal mind, and has no power to affect the spirit mind. That grows stronger and brighter and more active from the moment of separation, until it becomes so educated and balanced that it is the all-in-all of spirit life. I found it so, for I went to sleep in the mortal mind, and discovered at last that I was more vividly awake than ever."

THE JOY OF SPIRIT LIFE

"Joy is so closely united with service here that the two can scarcely be separated. You are thinking that this would not be so with the weak or the wicked. Possibly true. But through sympathy, understanding, teaching, or companionship, we learn that we help, and are joyous in that unseen help. Congeniality is the foundation of friendship here, and it leaves no room for friction or jarring notes."

"We cannot give a perfect description of this life; there are many things which we know are past your comprehension. But we are happy, and glad to be of service to those who need us; and service is half of our life here. By this statement we do not wish to make service seem unpleasant. It never is. For the joy of helping others is great; and too, it makes our own resting times or recreation times more happy."

'I suppose as spirit nature is higher and finer than human nature, so the joy of spirit life far exceeds that of mortal life.'

"Joy is joy wherever it comes. But here there is no background of sorrow or regret; no fear for the future. Many times our joy is an all-pervading contentment. Many times it is an infinite desire to give the world proof of the heavenly life. Sometimes a tender sorrow for those who cannot see or know. Can you understand?"

'I can see that those who believe that death ends all must have times of bitter grief.'

"Yes, the belief that human life is limited to a few short years, and beyond, only darkness,—the darkness which they have wrapped about their own souls."

THE SPIRIT BODY AND SPIRIT CONDITIONS

"We do have bodies, do use hands, arms and feet, can talk, can sing if we wish. These are the mechanical processes that are puzzling you. We cannot throw entire light upon it all, but perhaps it may help you to think of the material from which our bodies are constructed. This body is unseen by you, but is with you now, else how could you think, how could you move, speak, sing; or how could the emotions stir your heart and brain? Invisibility is not nothingness; nor is spirit substance invisible to us."

'We have been told that the spirit body could be contracted so that many could come into the room; that spirit could even balance on a needle point?'
"We know that is a problem with you. We could stand on a needle point because we could balance there and our weight would not destroy

the needle. It means lightness rather than smallness there. We can go into a room, many, very many at a time, because we can contract a little. Do you not sometimes fold your arms tightly, or draw your feet under your chair, to create more room? Something like this occurs with us—I mean analogous to that. We can fold ourselves more readily, and into smaller compass than the material body can do. But the effort is nearly the same. And no one feels crowded if one's arms and hands are contracted, or if the body is drawn into its smaller circumference.

"As for the rest, be assured that we do have the spirit counterpart of all the blessed things on earth: libraries, homes, flowers or lakes or groves. But we do not have the clumsy and awkward material things which are found necessary on earth. We do not need cars, or balloons or automobiles. Oh, no! Life is easier than that; and travel a luxury, and movement a delight."

'I suppose we are invisible to you?'

"Yes, you are nearly as invisible to us as we are to you, for our vibrations are too high to be of use in earthly material. But we do dimly perceive, and by practice we can get a fair idea of human beings and earthly material."

'It seems to us you miss much if you cannot see the beauty of nature here.'

"No, we do not. For we have the fairer counterpart here. Groves, mountains, lakes and valleys, all are here as we wish. They are a part of our spirit world and remain."

'Does your scenery always remain the same?'

"Perhaps not quite the same, for the reason that we can change its outlines if we wish: sometimes as you cut down a forest, tear down buildings to create a better view, or turn a watercourse out of its ordinary channel."

'When the first man went to heaven, he found a world ready for him, did he?'

"We believe so. We believe this spirit world is as much God's creation as the earthly world."

'Could it be that it was in a plain, crude form, and that spirit has transformed it throughout the ages?'

"Probably that is true. For instance, electricity has always existed, but it took man millions of years to find it and control it. There are still good gifts in that earth world of yours which man has not yet found. But he has been guided toward many of the hidden gifts of nature, and will sometime find and use the rest."

LIFE

'Can you tell us what life is?'

"We know nothing at all about it, except that it is. Life stands out and away from all argument as an ever-present truth, always manifesting its own truth. What we believe is that life is the gift of God, the one perfect gift among many perfect gifts which we may enjoy without even understanding."

"You are asking questions not even we who are here can answer. Perhaps farther on in our eternal life and activity we may know; but now, creation, infinity, eternity, from everlasting to everlasting: why? by whom? how?—these are questions which have remained without answer for unknown ages. Be content to wonder, to live, to enjoy, to serve. Let the higher knowledge remain to lure you on to higher efficiency and greater wisdom."

"We live the life, but do not solve its mystery. There is a Power beyond, a great, kind Power. Of this we are sure, more sure than ever in mortal life. We know that for us to be true, pure, unselfish, loving and helpful leads us toward that Power. I am speaking now of what we on this lower plane perceive. Do not think for an instant that knowledge is limited to this lower plane. Life and knowledge are progressive. We cannot begin here above what we had prepared ourselves for in our mortal lives. But the blessed law of progress is ours, always stimulating to new endeavor and new happiness. Every moment fills us with joy. We live—we love—we serve. Is this not enough?

"The heart of it all is love, happiness, service."

'In mortal life contrast seems necessary to complete our joy.'

"That is the human experience. Here there are varied forms of interest: new pleasures, new knowledge; and more far-reaching than these, the service we can give to those who need it. We have much work with the undeveloped, and much more of patient effort to win the really criminal ones into better and purer lives. So you see we have the contrasts after all. We do not suffer, because we know that all will be well at last. There is no hopelessness, you see."

'Does the thought of eternal life ever weary you as it does our finite conceptions?'

"Do not try to comprehend the activity and joy of eternal living and doing. This truth was not given to man to weary him; perhaps the comprehension of eternal existence is kept from the human brain purposely. It is a *tremendous thought*, almost too much for us here to realize, and altogether too much for the mortal brain. Let it go! Think of rest, or sleep, or even unconsciousness, if you prefer. All will be well, and your every need will be cared for. Never fear. Weariness does not exist for us."

THE HUMORIST

After a rather serious communication, our leader once wrote:—

"It may be quite a contrast to what you have had, but we would also like to bring to you a man who looks continuously at the humorous side of life. He was not a professional humorist on earth, but we think he missed his calling not to have been one. He is the life of our circle at times, never takes anything seriously, yet has the kindest heart of anyone.

He then took the pencil:—

"I am afraid your leader has put me on a pedestal, as it were, where I cannot make many motions without falling off. She is really the one who inspires us; she is the one we all look to for strength and guidance.

"We do not have disheartening tasks here, so my humor has little to commend it as an aid towards making life easier and happier. But I have always seen the funny side of everything, and often see humor when it is hidden from others. I am not going to crack any jokes in this writing, but I do want to tell the earth people that they should not be so long-faced and sad-visaged whenever the words *death* and *spirit* are mentioned. Life is continuous. Death is but an incident. Parting is only for a moment. And heaven is right at hand. If only this could be comprehended, we feel that life there would be more nearly one of contentment and happiness. We have so much to make us happy here that no doubt we forget many of the irritating things of earth. But we do remember that many of the circumstances that should brighten life there are either overlooked or forgotten, or in some instances never known."

AN EXPERIENCE

"I am not skilled in the use of the pencil, but I would like to express my pleasure at the messages that have come to us from earth. You know the old earth has never countenanced anything so mysterious before, and had I known of spirit communication when I was there, my life would have been far happier."

'Did you not believe in spirit communication?'

"Not entirely. How can a person believe in unseen powers when he is absorbed and narrowed by the seen? by the essentials of that life? I did not, at all events. And I approached the close of life with a fear that was almost horror. I was not wicked, as the world thinks of wickedness, but bound by the material and visible. And when the final test came I could not find the spiritual and unseen. So I passed. And my friends must have had little consolation in the thought of my entering upon new conditions."

'How did it fare with you?'

"I sank, out of extreme pain, into a sleep so gentle and peaceful, I think it would have been all right if I had never awakened again. But the waking came slowly, hardly consciously, until I finally knew that the terror was over, and about me were kindness and helpfulness. You probably cannot imagine those first moments of exquisite joy that I felt in the new life, a new opportunity to 'make good,' in a way, in a small way, but with such visions of larger opportunity before me that the life here has become truly the great adventure.

"I will go now; they tell me Mary and Dee are coming. Goodbye."

"We are here, Mary and Dee. Surprised enough at your recent visitor. But there is no harm in his communicating; and also his guides were with him. So you have had one more testimony, one more experience as to entering upon this unknown life."

A DAY IN SPIRIT LAND

"We might tell you of our wanderings today."

'How do you know it is day?'

"It is always light; but we do know when your sun hides its face from you, and we use your expressions of day and night which you would understand better than our continuous light and our limitless activity. For spirit sight does not require the sun."

'Where did you wander today?'

"We had a short trip to a nearby asteroid, for one thing:—life only at its beginning, the vegetation not yet ready for animal life. But we found it interesting. But we were not gone a great while, at least it did not seem long to us. Then we had a sort of informal meeting of our circle to decide on plans for study and travel and . . ."

'And what else?'

"Pleasure."

'Isn't all your work pleasure?'

"So it is. But we do sometimes give ourselves up to pleasures which have no object except enjoyment. Do you see? It is our pleasure to study; it is our pleasure to help others; it is our pleasure to go to libraries, or to other circles to watch their methods of teaching and helping. But once in a while we have—well—just that, a good time!"

'What do you do?'

"I do not think I can tell you exactly, because everything happens on the spur of the moment. Someone has an inspiration and we are all swept into it. It isn't cards; it isn't dancing; it isn't motoring. It is just the delightful letting down of our serious selves, just the happy interchange of thought and action."

'I am afraid we do not understand much of spirit life?'

"We know you do not. Neither did we before we came. But not all here is serious. We are not always studying big problems. We do have the delight of variety, of geniality, of the play of wit, the charm of perfect companionship."

DEE

'Dee, I was thinking today of the advance you have made since you have been on that side; how your conversation and communications come with so much firmness and conviction. You have grown much, I am sure.'

"I know that I have more knowledge; I feel that I have more power; I am certain I have many loyal friends. Who could help gaining confidence with this backing? We feel that all the more we have a duty to perform. As leaders of this circle, we feel that we must be able to guide them aright. We are studying and learning all the time, and the old saying, 'knowledge is power,' has much truth."

TIME

Written on my birthday:—

"We know nothing about birthdays here. You will forget them when you come. We never think of the passing of time, for it means nothing to us. You have no idea what a sense of freedom this gives. The feeling that one must do certain things at a certain time is gone, and yet it brings no sense of laziness. We have more ambition in every way. There is pleasure and interest in every moment. And then too, you can scarcely realize what it means to have no physical pain or weariness, no disappointment, no sorrow. Can you guess what it means?"

'You say you have no disappointments?'

"We have no disappointments that grieve. If either of you were to turn away from us, we would be deeply grieved, our love would have a shock. Yet we would know that it would pass and that you would return to us. Love here is not disappointed. Those who are meant for each other always come into loving companionship. Even circles are drawn together by mutual sympathy and love. Our circle is large, for many, many wish to hear from loved ones on earth. Yet not an alien thought, not an unwise criticism, not a word, question, or look, which is not in accordance and sympathy with the rest."

'How do you get any interest from opposing opinions?'

"We have plenty of those, but always in friendliness. So it is that we help each other; so it is that our plans grow more perfect; so it is that in varying suggestions, in the varieties of study and knowledge, in helping each other . . ."

The pencil stopped, but of course the intention was to show the way that harmony was attained.

The way the closing sentence was broken off shows the effort on their part to prevent errors in our writing. It will be noted that the last phrase was a repetition of the first one in the sentence. This was evidently noticed by them. Such a cessation in the writing often causes a long pause before the proper adjustment of power to continue can be attained. In this instance, it was near the close of the evening's writing, and it was not resumed.

PHILOSOPHY

"When you come to this side you will learn that philosophy is a greater study here than on earth; it is treated as a more comprehensive subject. We include all that you would class under ethics and religion. In fact we make it include all the studies of life as they pertain to the advance of the soul. It is not a subject for debate or controversy; just one of inquiry. It has drawn many of the great minds of earth into its study, as they have learned its value on this side. We have as a consequence many who are looked up to as great leaders in philosophical thought, and we hope in time to give you some of their conclusions."

THE INTERFERING SPIRITS

Two spirits were writing of their experiences there when the writing trailed off illegibly and stopped. Sis asked if what she had written was correct.

"No, that was not our writing. We are not the ones you called. We took the pencil when the others stopped a moment. We wish to write. How else can you understand the futility of trying to communicate with unseen friends? There is nothing, form, face, presence, to identify us. We who are unbelievers in the vain attempt to enlighten the world as to this life, believe you are better off to give it all up, and live out your earthly life without thought of the future, at least without belief in the presence in your dense earthly atmosphere of spirit friends."

'If it is so dense, how did you come?'

"We came through it all to enlighten you a bit. Give it up. It can't be done. We . . ."

Here there was a change in the writing as our leader, Mary, broke in:—

"Well, you have had a lesson in unbelief, haven't you? Don't let it disturb you, dear. We cannot help the interfering ones coming in now and then. But we believe you are not unduly influenced by them."
'Why do they do it?'
"Because they are not yet spiritually developed, and use the reasoning powers and beliefs that were theirs on earth."

At another time Sis had some trouble with such interference. That evening the following was written:—

"Mary and Dee are here. We know someone interfered today, and that the watchers drove them away."
'How did they do it?'
"We have to use the power of the mind. But its sharp thrusts are sometimes almost equal to dagger points."
'Is that quite in the spirit of love?'
"You are told to resist evil, are you not?"
'Yes, surely.'
"Well, when gentle means will not drive malicious forces away, we may use sterner ones, may we not?"

97

'I suppose so. They wrote your names?'

"We know, and that is the way the watchers knew them as malicious."

'They must make you a lot of trouble?'

"Not at all. Our work is one of love, and a desire to be helpful to mortals, and that drives away any thought of trouble or weariness."

'I shouldn't think you could keep watch of us all day long?'

"We do in a way; not always in close companionship, but a sort of magnetic wave which tells us where you are and what is needed."

At still another time some outsider wrote a few words. Mary explained:—

"Another spirit seized the pencil while we had turned away a moment. He was not criminal, just curious, and longing to try the experiment. The spirit world, you know, surrounds the earth, and spirits are ever wandering to and fro. We guard you from all evil ones, but this one seemed so anxious to try that we did not interfere for a moment. It is curious how amidst all the variety, all the attractions, and all the beauty here, the human mind slips back to its first home, and wishes to hear from the blessed old earth from which it came."

PRIVACY OF THOUGHT RESPECTED

Being told that most intercourse was by thought transference, we asked if all thought there was apparent to all spirits.

"We do not have our soul thoughts always on exhibition. There are unseen, holy, or loving places in each one's soul, that are sacred to one's self."

'How is it possible to be busy all the time?'

"If you wish rest and silence, the rest and silence are for you. In your mortal life the thought of continuous, never-ending activity is rather appalling. But remember that either rest or activity is for you to choose. Never doubt this."

THE NEIGHBOR SPIRITS

"We are members of another circle, but we are not used to writing yet, and cannot express our thoughts easily. But we would like to tell you of our life here, for we are busy and happy, yet with infinite possibilities before us. Think what it means to study any of the great sciences from this side! To study the stars and suns, for instance, the homes of multitudes of spirits. For each planet has a spirit zone surrounding it to which their own spirits go. There is, of course, intercommunication between the planets, and we are made happy by visitors from far-away zones. They tell us of a spirit life the same as ours, but of differing conditions in each planet; and that their bodies are made to conform to the conditions. Eyes can be made which penetrate darkness; bodies there are which delight in intense cold; ears may be attuned to the 'music of the spheres,' a poetic expression of mortal mind, but which means more than mortal mind has ever guessed."

OBSESSION

"Many do not realize that sin has no eternal life, that sin has to die, and the soul that persists thus comes into a purer life."

'But there are so many spirits who obsess earth people. These do not seem to lose their sin? Their sin doesn't seem to die?'

"Yes, that is the reason they become obsessing spirits. They cannot live in the pure atmosphere of heaven, and go of their own accord to find some life upon which they can fasten themselves and thus live out their evil existence.

"There is so much that is not understood. Life, human and spiritual, is so complex that it takes long to even understand it, to separate the good from the evil. Volumes could be written upon life and thought, upon unconscious motives, subconscious evils, but it would take more of a philosopher than I ever expect to be to explain and classify."

THE SCANDINAVIAN

"There is someone here who wishes to write, and thinks he can use your hand. We will help him."

"I was of a number who were anxiously studying the problem of the unseen. What we thought, what we believed, now seems astounding to me. We had worked out a transformation of our senses, affections, activities, until we were not even a likeness of our human selves. Strange, how the imagination can run riot and pose as actual unalloyed truth!

"Then I came over. What *could* happen, only to let me sleep in utter unconsciousness, while my guides tried to improve my condition? Years, many years, they tell me."

'Were you an American?'

"No, I came from across the seas. I was a Scandinavian as much as anything. We were what today might be termed a superintellectual group, and we prided ourselves in the destruction (mentally) of matter, of sensation, of intuition. Oh, Lord—what didn't we do to make ourselves super-human! Super-ridiculous, it seems to me now! I think there are a few of them over there now who deny all truth as commonplace, all nature as too simple, and try to institute a cult of something not understandable by any normal mind!

"Well, I have had my say. Can you guess how glad I am that I was brought back to a reasonable being, looking out upon a reasonable world, with everything making for happiness, freedom and advancement!"

'Is that all you wish to say?'

"Mary says he has finished his 'outpouring'; he is progressing, but is like an invalid who is on the road to recovery, but not quite well."

THE SOUL

"We wish to have you realize the spirit, the soul, behind all activities. When the physical body passes into the unconsciousness of so-called death, the emotions still remain. Thought is there, the power to hear, see, think, enjoy, are still there."

'The soul must be life then?'

"Yes, that in the large sense is true, but I would like to give it a little more definitely."

'But we have life here, so what are the eyes and ears for if soul is able to see without them?'

"The mechanism you have is fine, and is for use so long as needed by mortal life. But beyond this equipment is the more delicate one of spirit power. We here are so conscious of the difference, so conscious of the super-excellence of our spirit power, that we cannot help expressing this to mortals when the talk turns toward the activities of the human body, with its machinery for its limited stay upon earth. The spirit life with its spirit equipment is so enormously better and finer than the mortal, we would like to have you understand a little the advantages and joys of spirit existence. Never doubt them."

AN ACQUAINTANCE

In talking with a friend of childhood days, Sis asked:—

'Before your death had you thought much of the life beyond?'

"Only in the old-fashioned way, as the ministers describe it. My father had been a minister, you know."

'Did you find much to learn there?'

"Yes, I came with all the old orthodox teachings enveloping me, and it was hard at first to be rid of them, and know that the only hell is the one we make for ourselves, and that we need not endure it unless we obstinately hold onto our sins or our old beliefs. I was glad to be rid of both and start anew with hope and happiness and usefulness as my goal. Oh, I could tell you much of this life if I could find words for it all. But you may look forward to a happiness that will never fade, a kindly service for others that will give you untold joy."

'How can we serve there where all are so happy and all are so good?'

"Not all are happy; not all are good. Have you not seen or known of the selfish ones, the low-lived ones, the ignorant ones? Do not think that the mere fact of slipping out of the body entitles one to high thought, spiritual happiness, and the multitude of joys which are here. Mortals are fashioning their future lives right now. The diversity here is great. But kindness of thought and purpose, and a persistent belief in this life, will carry one far toward the happiness that awaits them here. I never had any idea of following my father's career there, but if I could go back now I surely would be an exhorter, a ... I don't know how to put it. But it would be such a passion for saving souls from all that is sinful, that life itself it would seem to me must be spent there in such service."

"It is difficult. People are so shut up in shells of their own belief.'

"I suppose so. I hardly know that, for I drifted easily along in orthodox fashion, believing I was safe, and ticketed for heaven without fail! Believe me, I found much to undo and unthink before my ticket was accepted! Goodbye."

FROM A NOTED PSYCHOLOGIST

The following purported to be from Prof. Wm. James: "I wish to tell something of my life here. I have written through several mediums there, but have not said much about my present advancement. We have so many things to interest us here that we forget sometimes that the earth people may like to know of ourselves as well as of our surroundings.

"When I first arrived my strongest desire was to try to demonstrate to the friends I left behind the fact that I still lived. In this I fear I was not very successful. As time passed and the attractions of this life began to manifest themselves to me, I was drawn away from my efforts to communicate with earth. I found many avenues of advancement, and all were so promising I had some difficulty for a time in making my choice. I have, however, finally chosen the lines in which I was most interested on earth. We have so many opportunities for study that were not open to us there, that any subject is found to be much larger than we thought it to be there. So I have found plenty to do in following the different trends in which these studies lead.

"We get different viewpoints on many of these because of our ability to understand some things that were beyond our grasp there. We see that many things which we looked upon as evils there, appear to us now as problems that were placed in our path for us to solve. We find that many things which we considered blessings were only some of the more cheerful events of our life. The real evils we did not fully understand, the real blessings have been left for this life.

"I have continued to study psychology, but only as an aid to understand some of the earlier phases of this life. Psychology here is not so important. But the study of philosophy, ethics and religion broadens out here, and comprises the larger portion of those studies which concern our future. We are always interested in trying to find some conclusions which we can apply to earth problems. The earth people need counsel in many ways, we think, and if such counsel can come from here with some authority, it may have influence."

SOME STRANGERS

"You do not know us, but the others are away, so we write."

'Do you belong to this circle?'

"Yes, and we love Mary and Dee, as they all do. We have not been here long, but we wished to try to write, so here we are."

'You say you have not been there long?'

"We think we have been *on this side* a long time, for we were unconscious longer than we could know. When on earth we were not in accord with spiritualism. We had heard of it, but only the common medium, the fortune-telling variety, and we felt superior to that. If we had only tried it out, had only investigated in an unprejudiced way, we would have come into the heavenly life without the dreary waiting in darkness and doubt."

'Had you no religion?'

"No, we were not even church members. We thought if we lived decent materialistic lives we would come into the heavenly one—if there was one, which we really did not believe. Our guides tried to help us, but we were buried too deep in our own beliefs, and had to suffer the consequences.

"Mary and Dee are the ones who finally brought us into the light. They led us to a spirit circle whose work it is to lead darkened souls into the light; and even then it was a long time before we could see clearly."

'You were helped by a spirit circle?'

"Yes. We could see a little, so Mary did not bother you with us. We know you love to help, but there are many here whose work it is to lead the doubting or lost ones into the true life. What a blessing it is!"

'You say you have not been long in this circle?'

"Not very long. We came when we graduated from the other circle."

'Have Mary and Dee arrived yet from their long journey?'

They had told us they were going on a trip to one of the planets.
"Not yet. They are gone longer than we expected.
'Maybe they are lost!'
"*No! Never! No such thing could happen here!*"
'Why not?'
"Because spirit perceptions are a perfect guide."
'I wish we could have those perceptions here.'
"It would make a change in the whole world; but that is not the law of evolution.
"We will go now, but we would like to come again and tell you of some of our experiences."

A SCHOOL FRIEND

An old school friend once made his presence known through Sis's pencil, although it was with much difficulty that she learned who it was. After the greetings, he went on writing:—

"Life there did not last long with me. But now I am glad to have been here all these beautiful years. I love it here, and can remain as long as I wish. The higher planes seem to my still earthly mind too spiritualized, too far away from the life as I have known it."

'I have thought that I would dislike to move on to higher planes.'

"You will be glad to know that you can spend centuries here if you wish."

'It seems to me that particular sphere must be very crowded?'

"It might be crowded, if illimitable space could be crowded. But you do not realize the immensity of heavenly space yet. We express things to you in language you can understand; but that language rather crudely describes our world or our life."

Later she referred to this friend when speaking to Mary, who replied:—

"We wish you could see him now with all the beauty of spirit development. He is no longer the bashful schoolboy, but aspires to high and fine ideals. You will see when you come how great are the possibilities in this life for growth and development of character. He is one on whom we can rely in helping others."

SPIRIT PLANES AND RACE PROBLEMS

"We have a visitor from a faraway plane, one who has never communicated with earth. He is surprised at the ease with which we give and receive messages, and, considers it a great advance from the life of fear and dread of this life which he felt there. He feels that it may be a great blessing."

'Do you mean that his circle is far away in advancement?'

"Partly that, but not entirely. The spirit world encircles the earthly world, and he may be thousands of miles away and yet be within the boundary of this world. The higher planes lie beyond us out in space. We say higher more as a term of advancement than of location."

'Do the different races gather in circles of their own?'

"Not necessarily. It is all a matter of congeniality. You cannot know the real worth even of some simple child of nature whose life has been spent in the wilds, or the desert places of earth."

'Are there foreigners in your circle besides the Chinese philosopher?'

"We have many visitors from other countries, but most of the members of our circle are Americans. It does not follow that it will always be so, for no nationality would be excluded. Nationality does make a difference at first. But study and experience, and the kindness that everywhere expresses itself, makes for unity and happiness."

'Do different nationalities show any difference in dress?'

"Not much. The clothing seems to express their thoughts or character, and Russian or Hindoo may express the same thought or character."

COMMENTS

An undeveloped spirit was brought to us one evening for help. The next evening Sis referred to the incident as very interesting.

"He certainly was an exception to the many whom we bring to you. But he is a type of many, very many, who come here with their mortal desires and plans still the only life they know. We talked with this one a long time after he could hear us, and he is at last convinced that he is here in the spirit world, and that a new life, a new adaptation to life, is necessary. It seems to us that when he at last actually understands this necessity, he will show the same persistence and determination to 'win out,' that had formerly made him a success in mortal life and earthly business. He will progress rapidly when once he is entirely convinced that the way leads to happiness, selfishly, probably, at first, but growing into spiritual insight by degrees until he becomes a fine worker here in helping others. This is our joy, to watch the advance of those who seem almost hopeless. You will love to help when you come."

SPIRIT SENSES AND EARTH VIBRATIONS

"All the senses belonging to the material human life, sight, hearing, etc.,—are of different organism here, fitted for the ethereal world in which material senses would be of no use whatever. You have been in contact with some of the souls who have come here without the

107

slightest preparation, and you know how helpless they are in spirit vibrations. Few indeed come who enter into heavenly glory at once. Often there is great disappointment. Usually they remain unconscious for a long time, during which their guides are sending messages to the quiet spirits, and endeavoring to prepare them for an awakening consciousness. But even then it is many times difficult for them to perceive through spirit vibrations. And this is why we appeal to our earth friends to help them through the lower earth vibrations, which they more readily perceive."

STAY BY THE TRUTH

An old friend says:—

"Stay by the truth as you have learned it. You have had wise teaching. Trust your guides, accept their words, for they are taught by higher instructors, and be glad of the wisdom that is given you. Try to think health thoughts, happy thoughts, and thoughts of helpfulness, and of the long, beautiful life here, which is rich in compensation for all the trials and miseries of that life."

THE "SUNSHINE" FRIENDS

Sis was standing outside in the sunshine when she unexpectedly felt an urge to write. Returning to the house, she took paper and pencil, and the following was written:—

"We are near you and wish to send some word. We are not Mary and Dee, nor any of your circle; just spirits wandering through the old familiar scenes of earth, and seeking to tell our friends that we live. We were of your country, America, but not known to you. We believed that the life of the individual passed away at death and became a part of the essence of life which pervaded all worlds, but without personal consciousness. We find life infinitely better, infinitely more joyous than we could have dreamed. We tell you this because we have several times been in touch with your thought, and see your occasional doubt of this life.

"We know of your circle and of their work. We know their earnest desire to prove themselves to the world. They do much to influence mortals, and they reach out to others than yourself in such efforts.

"We are two spirits, like an earthly marriage, as far as choice of companionship and love are concerned. Do you believe this to be possible with spirits?"

'Why not?'

"Yes, why not? For love remains. The difference between the sexes here is a difference in spirit attraction and understanding. Swedenborg was nearly right when he said man represented wisdom, woman love. But the wisdom and love known here are far beyond anything of the mortal kind."

The writing began to grow smaller and slow down, and Sis asked:—

'Are you leaving me?'

"It is you who are leaving. You begin to doubt and our power begins to fail. Why do you doubt?"

'Have you not known of mistakes that have occurred in our messages?'

"We know that mistakes occur. Not all of us are in touch with wise teachers. Not all are gifted in discerning the future. Are there not differences in power and intelligence among mortals?"

'Yes, of course.'

"Well, then, be wise; study your messages; accept the true; forgive or forget the mistakes. Goodbye."

"Have you nothing more?"

"Not this time. We will come again, but will talk with Mary first and see if she accepts us as occasional helpers."

At a later date they continued:—

"We are here again, your "sunshine" friends. We thought you would like to hear that we are taking notice of all the writing, and believe it will help many to know of this life:—That it is; and that they will come here at last, some in full belief, some in doubt, a few with joy. We came in ignorance, but not in any indifference, for we thought and grieved over our future. We had absorbed the materialistic philosophy, and it made the earth seem such a mistake, such a failure; so near to happiness, yet with true happiness always evading us. You will not have that outlook. Your coming will be one of joy, we are sure. Can you try, even more than you are trying, to make others enter into that same joy,—the joy of knowing that life is a gift that continues into a happiness not readily conceived in that sphere?

"We do not mean that all enter into that happiness at once. The malicious, the criminal, the careless, the unbelieving, the cruel, have a long and weary way to go. The old philosophers in their religion called it 'hell.' That may be a name for it; but, anyway, justice will not be cheated. Each must ... You cannot put on paper the fine analogy we were trying to give. But at any rate, life here is a continuation of the life begun on earth; and each one there is preparing his place here. ...

"Never mind. You know the subject is too big for us tonight."

THE ALL-WISE POWER

We asked how God's existence was proven to them.

"We know by the powers already manifested that no being less than the Almighty could create. We know through messengers from higher planes. We have the testimony from Christ, who is so near to the Highest, that he can tell us of His very presence. But perhaps most of all, is the absolute impression upon our inmost spirit that we are guarded, cared for, and raised into higher intelligence and purer life and joy by an influence outside ourselves. We know this with an assurance you can hardly understand; but it is more than sight, hearing or touch."

PRAYER

"We will start with the theme of prayer. Prayer on this side is altogether different from the wordings and ascriptions of praise of earthly communicants. We do not pray regularly. We do not have Sunday services in which are laws and regulations for drawing near to the Divine. We are filled at times with a recognition of the Great and Good and Loving Power above and beyond us. Our praise is more a spontaneous expression of love and joy that we are cared for by the Supreme Being, and we never doubt this or grow indifferent to it.

"This is our praise and prayer, a happy living recognition of the Creator, and the ..."

There was a short pause.

"I only wished to tell you how very far away we are from the ordered service, with its written hymns and prayer, or formulas for addressing the Most High. Love, spontaneous and ever-present love, and joy in that love, is our worship."

'You have no meetings then?'

"Sometimes we find ourselves in company with those who praise with us without formal preparation and without any law of praise or service.

"Our prayer is like the sunshine, or the fragrant wind.

"No, I cannot describe it. But it is an exquisite quality of joy, and expression of that joy, as we turn toward the Author of all joy."

At another time they referred to prayer as follows:—

"There is much liberty of expression here, also much difference of feeling. Many retain some of their former expressions. But if these are from the heart, they serve the purpose of bringing them near to the heavenly spirit. All do not think alike here. All do not serve alike."

DIFFICULTIES OF COMMUNICATION

"We have much difficulty in reducing the spiritual, the heavenly, the wonderful, into terms of human understanding. Then too, not all here are equipped with the power to perceive you of mortal life. Gifts are not all the same. On earth are the spiritual and unseen powers, and also the business and material opportunities. It is difficult to meet them all. We work half blindly, hoping that something of our thought and purpose may reach across the silence and help you to understand and to give to the earth people a new and satisfying view of this life."

THE JOKERS

Sis's pencil one evening wrote with almost lightning rapidity:—

"We are not trying much. This is not Mary. She was called away and we thought we would try. How do you like my penmanship? We think it pretty good for the first, but can do better after practice."

'Who is this?'

"Never mind. We are not malicious, anyway. But Mary would think us 'no good.' We would not measure up to her requirements.

"*She is coming! Goodbye!*"

Sis asked Mary who they were.

"Just jokers, and not much good, just as they said. But no harm is done. They will learn wisdom in time."

"I am glad there *are* jokers in heaven."

"You *may* be one yourself!"

AN OLD FRIEND

"This life is a great teacher. All our old earthborn ideas have to be restudied, and for the most part abandoned or revised."

'What is your work over there?'

"Oh, how I wish I could make you see it as I see it! But it cannot be described exactly. It is with the undeveloped spirits, even with the criminal, at times. But you cannot know how love can find entrance even into criminal lives, until you see its results here. I love my work, and there is much besides the teaching also. There is study of the most delightful kind; there is travel, which I longed for on earth but could never have; there is my home—my home, and I can hardly tell you how dear that is to me who never had one of my own on earth. And then through all, over all, surrounding all, is a peace and happiness which can only come from the ever present love."

'Do you mean love from Divine Power, or love of friends?'

"Both. We are conscious of a great surrounding goodness and care, and we are conscious too that this Care wishes us to be happy, happy beyond all happiness we had ever known before. And all here who have developed their spirit lives are filled with love and kindness and thoughtfulness for others. Can you understand a little?"

THE UNKNOWN COMMUNICATORS

"We are not your friends, Mary and Dee. We came because we heard your call into the silence. We are no one you know, no one who has used your hand before; but we are true in spiritual alliance, for we are of the same thought as your dear friends. We believe the life of the spirit must be service first, joy afterward. But no! That is not quite right, because service is always joy. The two move on together. And if the sad old world could learn the lesson of unselfish, unseeking service,—I mean unseeking of any return,—it would create a heaven on earth. There are saints over there, but their quiet self-sacrifice and loving service are scarcely noticed. The ruling passion for power, the ruling desire for riches to win this power, is almost universal. And the quiet saint-like souls who go on their way unobserved will grow more and more heavenly in character, and will become the nobility here."

'Is there difference in caste?'

"No, only one nobility, and only one entrance into its circles, only that of loving, kindly, unselfish service.

"That is our thought. We think your friends would be willing that we should write this to you."

'Yes, that is their creed.'

"We know that, and they are true and noble, you may be sure.

LIFE AND CHARACTER

"I am wishing to tell those on earth, who are struggling to learn what is the meaning of life, that it is the way one looks at it that determines its value. If one thinks of it as a time of sensuous enjoyment, one makes his life a thing of little worth, for such things have no value in the spirit world. If one looks at life as something to be endured

114

and to be gotten through with as soon as possible, he will form a character that has nothing to rest on here. He will have to create new foundations before he can advance. If one there believes that life consists in praying and preaching, that spirit is apt to want to pray and preach here; and in this world there are no churches or congregations that will respond as they did there, and the spirit has to learn that there are other things to acquire before the true life can be enjoyed. *When a soul on earth can realize that there are others there who need assistance, who will be the better for aid and sympathy, and can learn to feel that this aid and sympathy can be given by himself, he is in the way to create the life that will mean the most to him when his mortal life is over.*"

THE CARE OF LITTLE CHILDREN

"There are many who receive them, and they are very tenderly cared for until they awaken; that is, begin to see and hear by spirit means. We have watchers for them, like nurses in a hospital. And when it is noticed that one begins to show signs of wonder or curiosity, this one is taken to another place where experienced teachers look after them until they can understand that love surrounds them. This applies to those who were old enough on earth to have learned some things there.

"When they are awakened enough and experienced enough to understand the loving thoughts that are sent to their minds, they are examined carefully as to their different characteristics and as to their real mental ability; for we have learned that these manifest at a very early stage. No doubt this is much easier for us than for you, because we can usually read their thoughts quite readily.

"When they have been studied and cared for in this manner for a time, they are placed in groups under such teachers as will be best fitted for their special characteristics. We have found that we make astonishing progress in their education by following this procedure, and we have wondered why it is not more understood on earth."

'Is this Dee writing?'

"Yes, you know I have been teaching children nearly ever since I came. I have served in nearly all the various grades or wards. My classes have usually been those who were musically inclined, and it has been one of my greatest delights to see how readily many of them grasp the necessary ideas for a musical education. We have other teachers who are best fitted to teach those who seem destined for the loving missionary work; and others who know how to encourage any scientific tendencies that may appear. We are often astonished at the precocity of some youngster in the way of mathematics. But possibly this astonishes me more than it would some because I was always so backward in that way.

"With the younger children there is of course more time spent in the earlier care, while their little minds are developing sufficiently to receive impressions. But even this time is much shorter than it is on earth, and a tiny babe is sometimes in the study class with Marvelous quickness.

"It is such dear work that it attracts a very loving class of workers, and if mothers on earth only knew what tender care they always have, there would certainly be less grief over the loss."

'Does a babe that dies before birth continue to live there?'

"Yes, it lives, of course, and is cared for as tenderly as if years older. What difference does it make whether it is a few weeks old or many months old? It is a human being started on an immortal journey, which is only slightly interrupted no matter at what stage death may occur."

BELIEVERS IN MYSTICISM

"Many come here under the influence of the various mystic teachings on earth. These teachings, as you know, have more or less good at the bottom of all of them. And those who have followed them are still strong in their beliefs for a long time here, unless we can somehow show them that all goodness leads in one direction.

"We have circles whose members have been connected with such societies on earth, who act as missionaries now. They are especially qualified because of their previous knowledge. They mingle with the spirits whom they wish to help, and use their influence in persuading them that true spirituality is broader than anyone belief. They eventually drop their unnecessary rituals and peculiar ideas, and join those who are progressing.

"It is a necessary work here, for there are many who have adopted beliefs in theosophy and kindred thought, and they would all more or less group together and continue without further advancement here if there were not some outside influence to help them.

"The world little realizes how backward it is in acquiring spiritual knowledge. Nearly all would wander for a long time in darkness here were it not for the help that is given them. When you think of the multitudes coming all the time, and of the time it takes to influence many of them, you can get some idea of the multitudes of teachers and missionaries necessary here."

EVIL SPIRITS

"When those who have led evil lives first realize that they have left the earth life they are often very hard to manage because of their disappointment. They think of their earth life as gone forever, and they have no desire whatever for anything of a spiritual nature; there is nothing to live for, and yet they are alive. It is much the same as life imprisonment on earth, and knowing that it was impossible to get free. Their disappointment often turns to rage and they become for a time nothing but mad creatures. It is a very pitiful sight. Even when they begin to realize that their rage is useless, and they begin to listen to other spirits, it is still one of our most difficult tasks to arouse any ambition and get them started on the upward path. Then, if they have been the cause of much suffering on earth they have to pass through the stage of making compensation in some form."

'How can you be happy when you know some have such difficult paths to tread? And that there are so many of them?'

"We are happy because we can help, and also because we know that they will finally come into pure thought and kindly lives, and will shed their criminal desires as an individual might shed an old garment."

'How do they make compensation?'

"We think they go back to earth at times and try to undo their wrongs. They try to put good or fortunate impulses in place of evil and cruel ones, and sometimes succeed in bringing joy to those they have injured."

'It doesn't sound much like heaven when you speak of criminals there?'

"We are not talking of heaven when we speak of criminals. They are in the mental purgatories or spirit-hells the old writers imagined. There is no burning fire and no eternal punishment, but their mental suffering and final atonement are very real."

A SUNDAY SERMON

"We wish to affirm our belief that a new era, a new power, is coming to earth in the unfolding and renewing of spirit life through communication from this side. We are watching with longing eyes for nearness to us of earth friends, for renewing, or rather *creating*, spirit knowledge on that side. For we believe that if this life could be rightfully understood, and the knowledge acquired there that the earth life is only a preparatory existence, that life would then become a more important, a more beautiful experience."

'Who is writing?'

"We are two who loved, sorrowed, and were separated in our earth life, one of us preceding by a long time the other into the spirit world. We were not believers in spirit communication there, and I, who came first, sadly wondering, and filled with false theories and spurious wisdom, could not find immediate joy. At last she came, and all sorrow disappeared in the complete happiness and companionship of this life."

"Today is Sunday. Can you not give me a little sermon from over there?"

"Sunday! And a sermon! What should it be, what can it be, in this clear light, except *truth*, no other than truth, knowledge, great and glorious knowledge of this life and its never-ending joy."

'Does never-ending joy grow a bit tiresome, if there is no change, no contrast?'

"Never! An eternity of love! Happiness, increasing wisdom, knowledge, with an unknown and limitless universe for study! Satiety? Weariness? *No, never*! We cannot express it in any earth language. One must be here to realize its perfect satisfaction."

There was a pause of some moments. Finally Sis asked:—

'Is there anything more?'

"Yes, more, and much more, if only we could give it to you in mortal language. But to your thought we can only convey the sense of never-ending contentment and *progress*."

'A spirit of the time of Mahomet came to me once to say that all this modern conception of heaven is wrong; that there is no ecstatic joy, etc.'

"Yes, there may have been for him truth in those very words. For such souls may still be submerged in their own ignorance and false belief.

"*Let me tell the world* that human life in its short existence on earth may make its entrance here one of doubting ignorance, or even one of evil thought and feeling, for a time. This is true, because the divine law is one of personal freedom. Each soul can choose its own future. Each soul, still embedded in its human life, is choosing that future now. The old theologians, in their half-knowledge, described this life of the human soul as either a harp-playing multitude about a golden throne, or a descent into a fiery burning hell to be suffered forevermore. But this was only a human, emotional effort to describe the indescribable. The life here is the *reasonable result* of one's choice of one's character."

HELPING OTHERS

"Try for the best, always. And we believe the best is to acquire knowledge along spiritual lines. Live spiritually, think kindly, watch for opportunity to serve. There are so many who need help over there, and we here must work through human thought. Therefore we seek those who are ready to help us."

'In what way can we help?'

"First of all, in our judgment, is the understanding of this life. Not in the old ecstatic, symbolic way, but in the way of acquiring knowledge of the limitless opportunities for the human soul. We were not taught on earth that once past the gateway of death there was either opportunity or necessity for growth. Neither had we learned that service for others was one of the heavenly joys. Nor did we dream that through such service evil souls could be transformed into pure-hearted and wise-minded helpers!

"There must be an understanding of the wonderful possibilities here."

HEAVEN IS WIDE

"We are not your usual friends. We came to this circle to watch its work, and we find it fine in every particular. We are of another group, and have for our special work the teaching of new arrivals. You can hardly imagine the necessity of bringing the mortal thought into harmony with the heavenly. The mortal powers are for mortal minds, and are no longer used here. We love the effort to broaden their knowledge and turn their mistaken ideas of this life into true perceptions.

"Many appear to consider that there is a burning hell somewhere on or beneath the boundary of our heavenly sphere, and can scarcely give up the idea of everlasting punishment. But the only hell is in the thought or soul of the sinner, and he must be cleansed of evil thought, must be taught the first essential quality of heavenly life, which is *unselfish* service looking away from self, and growing persistent in the effort to help others.

"Heaven is wide and infinite in its possibilities. There are souls who do not come into realization of this life for a long time. Many seem to cherish the teachings, thoughts and tendencies of their earth lives, even when they are guided into better ones. But finally all go to their own place. That place may be with pure and beautiful spirits, or with the evil ones who will not or cannot forsake their sins for a time."

UNDERSTANDING LIFE

"The mystery of life there as well as here is almost beyond understanding. But the more we study it the clearer and more beautiful it grows. Do not be disheartened if you do not comprehend it in entirety. No one of us has arrived at that point yet. But take the blessings, yes, even the trials that come, knowing that all are in the way of education and progress. Can you not see already some of the beneficent effects of trial, disappointment and loss?'

'The wicked ones have trials and sorrows also, but it seems to do them no good?"

"Perhaps not as you see it. But sinners have to go through the fires of criminality, sin and sorrow sometimes before purification or advancement comes. Cause and effect. Cause and effect. That is progress, or that is the way to progress. No effort is lost."

UNCONSCIOUSNESS AFTER DEATH

"When death interrupts the action of the brain, all thought is then necessarily carried on by the spirit brain. It can sometimes do this at once, although usually only for a short time. In most cases it is unable to act at all for a while. (Presumably this is because it has always relied on the assistance of the machinery of the material brain, and lacks experience in acting alone.) This we think explains the first unconsciousness after death. After a time it receives additional power, as we all receive it, and then can function alone. It is often in a very dazed condition, however, for a longer or shorter period, and much lacking in reasoning powers. In addition, it may not have learned how to see and hear, thus still further limiting its action. So a spirit is frequently a very helpless being for a long time.

"It is when in this state that it can sometimes take possession again of a material brain and cause insanity. It is attracted by some force or impression, and clings to the new support like the proverbial drowning man catching at a straw. We do not think there are many cases where spirits willfully obsess a human. If they do, they are correspondingly difficult to dislodge.

"Some persons on earth have difficulty in thinking of abstract subjects. Such spirits are longest in comprehending the use of spirit powers. They are not always to blame. Many times they have inherited dullness that can never be overcome there, and are always much slower here. It is not the same as being materially minded. Many bright, alert minds think only of a sensual material life. They are delayed seriously here."

EVIDENTIAL TESTS AND PROPHECIES

In speaking of an event of which we had just learned, we were surprised to find that our friends on that side already knew of it. I said:—

"Well, you missed a splendid test. Why did you not tell us about it? I rather think that would have appealed to the public somewhat more than the messages."

"We know so surely of the life here that we forget the value of tests. We need someone to remind us constantly, for to us they seem foolish and unnecessary: like trying to tell one the sun is shining, when all can see the facts for themselves."

'Well, if there is anything to tell now, be sure that you do not overlook it.'

"There are no more events of that kind in the near future, but perhaps you may see some changes. But I will not foretell these; you must wait and see for yourself."

'Just how much *can* you foretell?'

"Not much. We can see circumstances and the probable results, and many are able to tell the future from them. But we are not gifted in that way."

'We have read of a number of prophecies, and have wondered how far such things were possible?'

"Some seem able to prophesy, but it is a psychic gift, or possibly a keen intuition, that can foresee results from certain conditions. We are not creatures of fate. Set that down as a truth not to be denied. We are free to live our own lives."

RELIGIOUS SERVICE

'Mary gave us a very interesting message once concerning prayer. Can you also tell us something of your religious services?'

"We have no church service, no creed, no rules, except the service of kindness and love. Our prayer is the spontaneous expression of joy and gratitude. But we constantly recognize an All-Wise, All-Loving, All-Pervasive Power, whom mortals call God. We recognize and serve this Power by trying to conform our lives and actions to this Protecting Love. If this Power so cares for us, why should we not use our own lesser powers for those whom we can help? We feel sure that this is the only acceptable worship of the Most High."

'By what name do you speak of this Power?'

"No name other than the Most High, the Great First Cause, or Loving Power, or other expression of confidence and loving worship. Christ is the greatest expression of that confidence and love, and we look to him as our teacher and elder brother.

"Cultivate the personal qualities of patience, gentleness, and helpfulness, and you will be cultivating your own spirit life."

'Where are Mary and Dee?'

"Out in space somewhere. I do not know their particular interest today, but there is always interest. Do not forget that."

'Interest enough for the whole twenty-four hours without sleep or rest?'

"Yes, for the whole twenty-four hours of day, week, month, years, ages, eternity—without the unconsciousness you know as sleep. Spirit does not weary. It has its passive times, but they are fraught with renewed strength and blessing."

A CONCEPTION OF GOD

We had asked some questions concerning their conception of God, and were told:—

"He is not limited to personality, even to the degree that we who are spirit are limited. If it were possible, I might explain a little more fully, but you could not at present understand. So try to be satisfied with the knowledge that God is present to the remotest part of the universe, and that God is a God of love, justice, and mercy. Never doubt this. The more spiritual we become, the nearer we grow to that blessed spiritual presence, and the more nearly we approach, the more our spirits are filled with love, awe, and reverence. Be content to serve with the love of God in your heart, and sometime your knowledge will be perfected."

And again:—

"It would be difficult for you to even realize the absolute existence of the Creator of all things. Material form is not his, nor perhaps spirit form even, as we know it. But His influence is everywhere. Be content until your soul is illumined with further understanding. We here do not see God as a person, or even as a spirit. That vision belongs to the spiritually advanced and illumined ones of higher spheres."

A question had also been asked about the Lord's Prayer:—

"Christ had this inspiration. It is one of the perfect ones, unalloyed by mortal thought. Use it, knowing that it does avail with the Father of us all; for God, the Father, is always near and always ready to help. We do know God, the Father, better than you, but he is a spirit so ethereal that we of the lower planes do not see Him. But we feel his influence far more than you, because we are farther removed from the material senses."

DESIRE FOR RECOGNITION

"We grow impatient here at times at the delay of earth people in their recognition of our presence, especially by investigators whose word would have much authority if given in our support. We have given the world proof after proof, and yet they want still more. We think the time has come for us to insist that they give their attention to the vast accumulation of evidence, and make some use of it.

"No honest investigator has really denied the reality of our manifestations. But it is so difficult to get them to publicly admit it. We are trying to use our influence now to have someone make a thorough analysis of the quantity of material that is in their hands, with the determination to show that there is sufficient to supply a firm foundation for a spiritistic belief."

We said that Prof. Richer had made some analysis of that kind, but had failed to arrive at a spiritistic belief.

"We know. We hoped he would be the one to do it. We think there are several others who will be amenable to our influence, and we hope for some show of success."

FORGETTING

We were talking over the question of evidential matter, realizing that most evidence would be connected with material things. I thought it probable that under the conditions of the new life, they forgot many things of this life. Turning to the pencil, it wrote:—

"We are listening. We do forget our earth lives, with all the appointments we treasured while there. You can hardly realize the complete transfer of interest when the change is made from the earth life to the spirit existence. We are hardly conscious of the earth life, for the change in every particular is so great, and every moment here is so filled with joy, or study, or care for others, we do forget—forget everything except the love we bear for the dear ones there."

SELFISHNESS AND SIN

"The one truth we are all trying to send is the influence the mortal life has on its immortal existence. We wish the earth people to know that there is no hell except that which the mind has created within itself. We wish them to know that the condition of the wicked here is one of unhappiness and misery; and that only they themselves can release them from the mental torture of their own creating: only a complete abandonment of sin and selfishness can open the doors to heavenly happiness.

"Do you imagine that an earthly life of selfishness and sin can suddenly change into a life of purity and love? Let us assure you that no such change can occur, but must be worked out patiently and slowly by the sinner himself. And it may be years, or lifetimes, or even centuries, before the awakened one can replace sin and selfishness with loving service for others.

"Make this clear if you can, and help mortals to awake to the truth that selfishness is the foundation of all sin, and must be overcome before one can enter into the joy of heavenly life."

THE COMMUNICATING CIRCLE

'Does your circle have other interests than communicating?'

"Yes, of course. You don't think we are bothering the old earth to speak to us all the time, do you? We do call ourselves a communicating circle, but we meet for all sorts of discussions, and also for just friendly social life—visiting, you might call it. We separate at times and go our own various ways, and then meet again and relate our experiences, ask for advice perhaps, or maybe have some humorous story of adventure to relate. Do you believe this last?"

'It doesn't sound much like the old orthodox idea of heaven!'

"Not much it doesn't! And we are glad. Heaven would scarcely be a place of endless enjoyment for us if psalm singing and harp playing were to occupy an eternity of time."

'Can you tell us what you have been doing today?'

"Yes, we would like to, if we can measure a day in your kind of time. We went 'out in space' with a teacher for a time, then returned and found a wonderful concert taking place in the temple of music. Then we went to look up some friends, 'making calls,' you would say, and afterwards listened to a lecture on—well, on etheric, no, thought waves. This took most of the time until we got your call and came here."

'How did you get the call?'

"Just a thought call. It comes like an impression on the brain."

'How many are here?'

"Not all the circle. Many were away with other occupations or with other friends. So chiefly your most intimate friends are here."

LAST CENTURY EXPERIMENTS

We were talking with a man who had been on that side for many years, and knowing that he had been concerned with the wave of psychic phenomena that spread over the country some seventy-five years ago, we asked him to tell us about it. He replied:—

"There was much real mediumship, but all along material lines. I was interested for a long time, but it did not lead to any better or higher life, and did not impress me as being at all heavenly, so I gave it up at last. No one knew the cause of the manifestations, and all were hunting for some explanation. I could not see any good arriving from it, and I tried to account for it in some logical material way. But it never was explained satisfactorily to me until I came here, and could see for myself just the influences and experiences that could go forth from earthbound spirits on this plane."

'I think I have been told that at times you heard sounds like the steps of a dancer, a man whom you had known?'

"It was more of an impersonation. I cannot explain it just as I wish. But it was not my friend, only an imitation by the medium of some characteristic of his. He had not at that time come into a very advanced state, but could possibly have sent an impression of himself to the medium. I have not learned the truth, as he has advanced to a higher plane now, and I have not talked with him about this appearance."

There seems to be a hint here that some physical manifestations may not be directly caused by spirit; they may be caused by suggestions from a spirit source, and carried out unconsciously by the medium.

DEATH FROM ACCIDENT

In talking with a man who had died from an accident, we asked if he could tell us of his passing. Immediately Sis's hand and pencil were shaken violently. She experienced a cramping pain and an impression of gloom. After a little, the pencil wrote with emphasis:—

"That is awful to remember even now. It happened so suddenly, and I was alone and helpless. It was so terrible that the suffering came with me to this side. But it is all over long ago. My spirit finally came into peace, and I was met and cared for with great tenderness, and my life now is so happy that I forget the rest. But the suffering I endured made me the special care of friends who tried in every way to blot out the memory of the pain and agony, and lead me into peace and happiness. You have asked of the occupations of the angelic ones here. Can you not see here one more service in caring for such spirits? The earth memory still clings to them for a time, and therefore they are the more tenderly cared for and led away from all painful thoughts."

'Is there compensation for such suffering?'

"All pain is lost at last in the final peace. But if there are those who cause the pain, I mean the deliberately cruel ones, their atonement here is sometimes through much pain and suffering."

'I meant compensation for accidental suffering?'

"The suffering of earth is so short compared with the eternity of bliss, that all thoughts of compensation are lost in the very reality."

OUR FIRST EXPERIENCES

Four of us were together one evening, and we asked Mary if she could tell us what would be our first experiences if we should suddenly come there together from any cause.

"That is a question not easily answered. First, the unconscious period, which might be long or short according to the spiritual advancement of each. Then the awakening, and then, ah, then! the beauty, the loveliness, and the surprise! We think then a quiet enjoyment, a quiet receptivity, the while your spirits were becoming accustomed to the light and glory.

"We know that you would soon gladly take up two occupations: the one of learning the laws of spirit life, the accustoming of your souls to the new atmosphere; and the second, the eagerness for two things— to send back word to those on earth who loved you, that *heaven is heaven after all*; and then soon the law of spirit life would possess you, and study for improvement, for knowledge of this wonderful life, and then the immediate desire to draw toward you, and toward heavenly delight, those whom you loved on earth."

'Who was writing that?'

"Dee wrote this time, for her own experiences came back to her suddenly, and the glad surprise which possessed her when she first became conscious."

THEIR "USUAL" LIVES

"You know our lives here have become for us the *usual*—all its brightness, its knowledge, its wonder, its variety, its purity, and yes, its holiness. Only do not think of that word in its usual acceptance. But all these are our *usual* life."

WHAT WE CAN DO

A friend with us asked them to tell us the best way to do our part in making the truth known.

"You may find many things to do. It is thought here that most people on earth are too afraid of adopting the idea of a spiritual life. We think that this fear is not warranted. It is not necessary to parade such virtues. *If one will only live a life of helpfulness, of thought for others, of kindness wherever possible, he has made a great beginning.* And if many could do this, the world would soon notice the result; and the attention then attracted would not be annoying. From this would come the publicity that is necessary for the spread of any new thought or idea. It should not be a very disagreeable task to experiment. When a few can be near enough to each other to bring the sense of support to the actions of each, then the greatest difficulty is overcome.

"We do not look for great things to be accomplished in a short time. We do feel that a beginning should be made, with a definite object in view; and we are willing to await results. We believe that each truehearted believer in the nearness of spirit life, and who comprehends the beauty of this life, may become a center from which may radiate a power for good that will be far greater than you at present realize."

This subject was brought to our attention at a later date when some strangers wrote:—

"We wish to tell you of our thoughts. We hope for greater activity among the believers in spirit life. Can you not form some thought union?"

'Just what do you mean by that?'

"We mean that those who are with us in desire can form a thought union—rather, a purpose to accentuate that thought until it becomes action.

"We are among those who on earth did not believe in this farther life. We lived a material existence in a material world, and looked forward to the long, long, unbroken sleep. When we came here we did pass into a long sleep, but awakened to conditions and possibilities for which we were not prepared, and another long time of unhappiness awaited us before we began to see the orderliness of spirit progression. Then we began—perhaps you might call it the first letter of the spiritual alphabet. And from the first small letter has come the whole perfect and beautiful story. But years have been wasted, worse than wasted, because we absorbed the time and power of beautiful spirits who might have long been in happier pursuits. So, for the human being himself, and for the beautiful spirit that might be called to watch and teach the stupid soul, I ask more light over there, more preaching of good tidings, more gathering together of the needy unspiritual ones for teaching and leading, that they themselves may become a power for good. Try for power. Try for unity. What is it the Bible says about 'when two or three are gathered together, etc.'? Try it. Organize. Teach and preach the beautiful truth of immortal life."

And Mary added:—

"We are so desirous of having these truths put before the world that we cannot rest content until we see some concerted effort made to influence others."

SPIRIT SIGHT

Ordinarily the presence of other people interferes with passivity sufficiently to prevent writing, or at least good writing. But one evening some intimate friends were with us, and we asked Mary if their presence was detrimental.

"Mary says, it is an aid, and if you could continue for a time we think it would be a very great help. It takes time to harmonize the forces of several persons, but your friends will be easy to bring into perfect harmony."

She was also asked if they could see the material things of earth sufficiently to make traveling about the earth's surface a pleasure.

"It is not easy. Some seem to have the ability to see their intimate friends and their surroundings, especially when they first arrive here. It is a special gift if they are able to continue. In a few cases the gift *has* continued, and so a few spirits can see the material things of earth quite well. We ourselves see very little of it, not enough to get any pleasure traveling about its surface. It is a gift that can be cultivated with some. But here again, very few do so, because the attractions here are so much greater that there is little incentive."

'What do you do there when things go wrong, and you get 'blue' and discouraged?'

"It doesn't happen! We do sometimes wish we had more power, that our influence could travel farther, or that we ourselves were of greater influence. But this is always met by our guides or helpers by encouraging words and helpful and loving advice."

MARY's MESSAGE

"We are here and anxious to write."

'Why anxious?'

"Because we wish to send the truth of this life to earthborn friends, that their influence may go out to others and win many souls to heavenly life. Do you see that unbelief is increasing on earth, that multitudes are following after the gods of riches, pleasures, and power? We here are asked to use our influence to help stem the tide of atheism, of wickedness, of worship of wealth, power, and position. These things are in the way of pure spiritual life and truth. They are bearing down upon the earth with malicious force, and the wicked ones here are glad, glad that this is so."

'Mary! That is very emphatic for you!'

"Well, we have just had a lesson from one of the great souls here, that we must bend our energies to help the cause of truth, purity, and righteousness on earth; and we turn to you to help."

'It is so difficult. What can we do?'

"Wait, and the knowledge will come to you. Make the world believe in this life as a continuation of that. Do not preach the old gospel of golden harps and pearly gates for the few, while uncounted multitudes are bathed in the fires of hell. We must influence! We must bring wiser thought to earth.

"We have preached a sermon, but we were full of the subject, and felt that it was a good time to pass it on. You little realize the need for work to make the people understand. We see the effects of this wave of materialism in the souls who come to us. We have no trouble with those who have some spiritual thought. But how few these are! It is sad to see the multitudes who linger near the earth, drawn by no forces except the material ones that ruled their lives while there. We cannot reach these multitudes easily, and many we cannot reach at all. And we grow sad at the thought of the long years of darkness and misery that so many must endure. You must try to put the truth before the world, if not personally, by means of books and papers."

GUIDES

We have many times been told that everyone on earth attracted some spirit who tried to influence and guide their charge through all the vicissitudes of the earth life. This caused us to ask if even a criminal had such a guide.

"Yes, always. All have guides. But it is sometimes difficult for the guides to impress their charges. Usually in such cases there is more than one guide and influence. It would be very difficult for anyone with high spirit development to be obliged to stay near an ignorant and coarse-grained individual."

'Is one's guide always present?'

"That is not necessary. In the first place, a guide, to be a true guide, will know the character, the possibilities, in the life of his charge. These will be like a chart to inform him when and where he is needed. To be constantly with one mortal life would interfere with the progress of the spirit, and it would not be well for the mortal to be so guided. We do not stay with you all of the time, as you know. But faithful watchers let us know immediately if we are needed."

'Is this true with others?'

"Yes, this is always so. A guide, to be a true guide, must advance, must grow spiritually, must have much knowledge and quick perception, and must endeavor to lead the human soul to higher planes. This he could not well do if his own life and education were stationary."

Mary had spoken once of referring to her guides or helpers, and we asked if they themselves had guides.

"I did not use that word in exactly your meaning. But we do look always to an influence higher than our own: sometimes from another circle, sometimes from another plane, and in the last analysis, perhaps to Christ. And beyond this lovely and loving influence, to the Father of us all, to the Highest Spirit, whom you call God."

THE UNBELIEVER

"I feel now as if I had been such a blunderer. To think of us over there—poor humans chasing around after little specks of happiness we hoped to find, and missing a universe of joy in our future! We should think, and as far as possible, live this life before we come here."

He had been a golf player here, and was asked if he played it there.

"Not that. But you needn't think we are a psalm-singing, harp-playing lot of people over here. Joy, pleasure, study, helping others when we can. Strange, that even over here there are souls living in poverty of—well, a lack, utter lack, of happiness because of their own unbelief! I was one of the unbelievers there, but I did not stay so. One glimpse of the glory, and my soul was filled with joy; and never again has doubt assailed my mind.

"You did not know, I guess, how far my unbelief went. But I could not find God anywhere in my business, and of course I could not find any immortality, or soul, or spirit life. Fool that I was!"

SWEDENBORG

Mary was asked if they knew of Swedenborg on that side. She replied:—

"His influence is strong here. He long ago ascended to higher planes of thought and speech, but he is looked upon as a great scholar and a pure and strong influence. Mary thinks he has his greatest influence among the *intellectually spiritual*. You know, I hardly belong to that circle, but I can still admire and learn."

We spoke of the doctrine that Swedenborg had formulated.

"Mary says, we here have a far simpler doctrine, as you know. Principally, kindness to all, and service wherever possible. But we realize that many need the stimulus of a more involved creed or doctrine, and Swedenborg can certainly supply this need."

She was asked about his teaching that Christ was God, or a part of God.

"You will not hear that, we think, at least from those who have been here long enough to enter into the real truth of this life. We look to Christ as the most perfect example of God's love and wisdom that ever lived on earth. We think he was especially gifted in expressing the love and wisdom of the Most High, but we believe that he never claimed to be a *part* of God."

FROM THE CHINESE PHILOSOPHER

"If science finds means to hold the faith of the world, it will rule the world. We mean that spiritual ideals are opposed to pure science and can never be brought into combination with it. We see the two proceeding side by side, each filling a need in the world, and each contributing to its advancement. So we can say:—

"Preserve your ideals; they are rocks that serve to anchor your faith when science threatens destruction."

He then went on with a few rather pointless sayings or aphorisms, and I could get little meaning to it until the closing paragraph:—

"You see, I have tried to give some that are different from what you have received before. There are two reasons for this: one, to show that an outside influence dictates them; the other, to avoid an expectant attitude on your part."

IMPERFECT COMMUNICATION

"So far as we know there is no one on earth who is communicating with unseen friends who does not at some time fail of the truth. The conditions are difficult. The human mind acts so easily and in such unexpected ways. But we still think that much good goes to earth, and that with all its mistakes spirit communication is the great hope of the world. The power of the church has grown limited. The great public mind is very indifferent to religious teaching. The indifference to the various creeds makes some new and powerful influence necessary to draw life into consideration of and preparation for the eternal existence."

138

MESSENGERS

One evening we asked if they could find a lady who had passed to that side some fifteen years ago. Mary said she would send out messengers to inquire. After a few moments of quiet, she continued:—

"We cannot find her. Our guides think she has gone to higher planes. I called messengers and they went straight to headquarters (did you know we had this help?), but could get no information, so they returned. It is generally useless to try to find one under such circumstances, as we do not ascend to higher planes freely from this one."

'Do you ever under exceptional circumstances find anyone when on a higher plane?'

"We try, but seldom succeed. Sometimes on rare occasions someone from such planes comes to us for a moment, or sends their influence, just as old-time philosophers or teachers may occasionally send their messages to us, although they themselves cannot come. We have explained to you that those from higher planes cannot easily exist in this denser atmosphere or condition."

THINKING SPIRITUALLY

Four of us sat together one evening when Sis took the pencil.

"Mary and Dee wish you all good evening!"

We replied and expressed our pleasure at their presence.

"You are all seeking the same truths, that of spirit life and spirit occupation. We have tried to give you news from here, but you must know that words are inadequate. We can only say again, think spiritually, act spiritually, and trust us to help you on your way."

'You say, think spiritually. Can you tell us just what you mean by that?'

"Mary believes, first of all, the recognition of the Great Wise Power, whom you on earth call God. Then think of the life on this side and of how best to prepare for it.

"Dee says, you know when we were preparing for our European trip, we read books of description, we prepared our wardrobe, and our thoughts were turned to the prospect before us. Suppose you apply this preparation spiritually. There are many, many books to read, not only those of earthly writers, but also those whose inspiration has come from here. Then we might find a parallel in the thought of the clothes as compared with spirit clothed in unselfish thought, and in the white robes of spiritual intuition, and spiritual help for others. ... No, I am not expressing this well. But you are good at guessing and will see my meaning. Dee."

SPIRIT CLOTHES

The reference in the preceding paragraph to clothing caused us to ask what they were wearing as robes now. Dee replied:—

"Mary has on her usual white and glistening robe. Mine (do you remember the colors I loved?), sometimes a pink, sometimes a lavender, but in delicate shades not known on earth."

Someone of our number facetiously remarked:—

'And you do not have to send to the cleaners, or keep extras hanging in a closet!'

"Not much! Thought, or the thought method, performs the work. We can throw them aside and assume others at will. What has be learned at even earthly séances? Has he not seen the seemingly perfect materials dematerialize?"

This referred to a time when the questioner had seen the clothes on a materialized spirit change before his eyes from an ordinary suit to a military suit with brass buttons.

I asked how the clothes of the newly arrived were supplied.

"They usually appear in white, because that is the spirit color."

'Who supplies them?'

"We think that belongs to spirit appearance. I should except, however, the criminal ones who come over steeped in their own wickedness. They appear in dark colors, sometimes quite repellent."

Some of us apologized for inquiring so minutely about such things.

"It will help when you come. There will be no strangeness for you over here, we think. Thought prepares the way, and you will all feel that you are just coming home."

'Do your descriptions really convey the reality, so that we can at once understand, or are such things practically indescribable?'

"It is indescribable in a way, but in another way it will all seem as you have thought of it: a new and beautiful home, loving and lovable friends, with a friendship across which no shadow ever falls."

THE SPIRIT HOME

In the previous volume, *Spirit World and Spirit Life*, Dee gave a description of the home which she and Mary occupied. Reference is again made to it in the following:—

"When you come to this side you will be met by loving friends, and you will soon acquire your spirit powers. In this way you will

141

be quickly introduced to the spirit home that is awaiting you. We only wish you could see it now. You have a description of it, but you little realize its beauty. We have changed a few things since that was written, but it is still much the same.

"You would think we were wonderful architects, no doubt. But you must remember that we have so much help in everything we wish to do, that we can acquire a ripeness of knowledge on such a subject in a time that you would consider marvelous. We have no way of picturing the comfort, the 'hominess,' of our abode. It is all as our thought and desire have constructed, and in this way reflects our own personalities. We sometimes say that a home resembles its occupants, for it represents the character so truly."

THE SCIENTIFIC CIRCLE

"We visited another circle some time ago where they are especially interested in scientific work. We found there a number of spirits who on earth were noted for their scientific achievements, and they have formed a sort of scientific society here. It is through their influence that some of your important inventions have been perfected; and they are trying to impress further ideas on your workers there.

"It is a wonderful circle, and is doing much to help the human race. But if this circle under Mary's direction can only succeed in getting *their ideas* into the minds of mortals, they will be achieving still greater results. For the human race needs spiritual uplift far more than it needs further scientific discoveries."

SPIRIT COMMUNICATION

"I am here as a guest in this circle, and have learned for the first time that communication with mortals is possible. I never believed it on earth, and my progress here has never until now brought me in contact with anyone who knew of such work. I am much pleased to know of the possibility of sending information back to earth people. We undoubtedly make more rapid progress in the acquirement of knowledge than do those we left behind. And if we can help them to understand a little of what we have learned, it may help the world through some of its difficulties.

"We always think of the effect that our knowledge may have on the human race, but I had always supposed that our spirit influence was the only means of conveying these benefits. If we can talk directly with earth people, it should be much easier to put some of our ideas into effect."

'Yes, if only we could make these people believe them. But the opposition to such things is difficult to overcome.'

"Yes, I suppose so. It is easy to forget the obstinate ignorance of many there. It should not be so. Why do they believe in a future life, and yet have no concern about it?"

'That is a mystery to be solved. They usually seem to wish to put such things out of mind.'

"Well, so much the worse for them. It should be an attractive idea. But no doubt some fear that they should be leading different lives if they held a belief in its continuation after death.

"You have much wise teaching from this circle, I am told. I hope you can get it before the world. It certainly was needed when I was there, and if reports are true, matters have grown no better in the twenty years or more that I have been here."

THE GREAT ADVENTURE

"We would like to fill your minds with the immensity of the world here. We would like your help in trying to impress mortals with the thought of this life. And then we would like to give you some of our impressions in regard to life—the mystery, the enticement of it all. There is so much before us that life becomes the 'great adventure.' There is no staleness, there is no weariness of mind; and day by day, vista by vista, time by time, brings us new joys and new experience.

"We feel that if the knowledge of this life, with its joys and its penalties—for penalties there are for misspent and sensual lives—if these could be known and believed, it would change the earth life to a wonderful extent."

GLEANINGS

In an evening's communication the pencil often records material on a number of different subjects, and in a manner which makes a division of it according to topics almost impossible. So the short articles on the preceding pages convey much varied information, yet seem almost impossible to classify. Even the title by which each is designated does not always indicate the content. After they were transcribed, the following paragraphs remained; and it seems reasonable to include them under the above heading.

"Here is a teacher who is prominent here, and who is very successful in helping the physically weak. He says:—

"Start the day with deep breathing for five or ten minutes. Then take passive exercises with the thought of spirit control: that you are simply the expression of spirit life, and should think of it as perfect in every way. If pain comes, or any discordant physical condition, look not only to spirit life on this side for help, but to your own spirit life; for that is the perfect mechanism given to you to carry you safely through your earthly career. If you will follow this steadily and continuously, you will see an improvement in health, and it will measure in proportion to your persistence and your faith."

We asked for one who had lately passed to that side, but they could not find him.

'Could you not find his guides?'

"Not necessarily. Do not forget the immensity of this spirit world, and the millions upon millions who come. Can you possibly understand it all? The coming, coming, coming of souls into this life is not readily comprehended. We have to have a very complete system of guides, messengers, and mediums even sometimes, to trace the unknown ones whose friends on earth are seeking for them. We are glad to try, but say this, that you may have patience while we use our skill in finding the unknown one."

'Is this Mary?'

"No, not Mary or Dee. But I have been on many a search for spirits whose friends were calling for them, and I took the pencil to explain."

"Please try to think back to the beginning of life, from the earliest form of life up to man. Has not the progress always been upward? Then try to believe that the same upward trend, the same possibility for developing fine and still finer personalities still exists. Upward, ever upward, is the line of evolution."

'Where will it end?'

"We do not know the end. Infinity is still hidden from us. We are not developed enough to even conceive what lies before us. But be sure of one thing, absolutely sure: You will never miss your human body, nor want to exist in one again.

"You have made much progress in your study of psychic subjects, and we hope you will continue to study, for you have scarcely begun yet. It amazes us to learn of writers there who push aside all such matters as foolish, thinking that they know all about them. We here really know very little yet, but how much less the earth people know! It is a study that is actually the study of life itself. And when will such study end? It is like casting aside the truth of existence itself. You will learn as you progress in your studies, that all psychic phenomena are connected with the problem of life, and should really never be entirely separated from the study of life. Many there think that life in the material world is all. But even with them life stands preeminent! How much greater it appears when viewed in the light of immortality and eternity! It is the most important thing in the universe."

"I am glad of this opportunity to tell you of the need of the world. I have been given glimpses into the mind and soul of many over there, and know that many 'hunger and thirst' for knowledge, for evidence of this life. They follow blindly the teachings of the past. Also I have seen the indifference to the future of many human beings, and know that they need a jar, a shock, to bring them into a realization of the briefness of the earthly life, and the eternity of the future existence. We hope for much from this coming to us of the psychically gifted ones, and gladly give to them what we may of teachings of this life. The need is great. Do not let discouragement make you pause."

"Try to give what you can to the world. You grow discouraged over the bigness of it all, the immense changes which would come to human thought, if our words could be believed. Do not try to estimate your influence, or grow discouraged because you can see so little result. Remember that Christ himself had to depend on twelve apostles for belief, friendship, and spreading His truth before the world. Go on! Do what you can, and let us send our words across as we can.

"Heaven is here, life is here, happiness is here, and nothing to ever disturb us more. Why not be happy and joyful?"

'How can you be happy when there are so many who are in misery there because of ignorance and crime?'

"We do not see them, but we know that in time they too will come into happiness. Is not that enough to be grateful for? The old idea of hell was one of eternal punishment, never-ending sorrow or suffering. What a horrible mistake the old preachers made! How was it possible to put such a black spot on religion?"

"We hope you will keep every high and spiritual thought and impulse that have come to you. We here in this circle have not tried for physical phenomena, nor for messages for mortal curiosity. We wish to lead you toward the higher life, for it is great, so wide, so deep, so satisfying, that all else seems puerile."

PART II

UNDEVELOPED SPIRITS

UNDEVELOPED SPIRITS

It is customary in this life to spend many of our earlier years acquiring an education in preparation for the years to follow. Most people, however, seem to proceed as though the eternal life beyond—if there is such a thing—will take care of itself. If any preparation is necessary, there is time enough to do it in the afterlife, they seem to argue, or else they believe that conformity to some creedal dogma is the essential requirement. There is time enough, of course; but we learn that dogma and doctrinal observances may hinder rather than help, and that very many have to go through the preparatory course after arriving on the other side. If this were all, the matter might not be quite so important. But we also learn that it is not necessary to waste these first years there in that manner, if certain things are done in the earth life and certain other things avoided. The education, if acquired in this life, is short and easy, and, moreover, is a great aid to a successful life here. It consists of following as nearly as is practicable the teachings and example of Christ—just the life that we as Christians are supposed to follow.

But evidence from the life beyond indicates that many, very many, either through ignorance or through willfulness, have not been as successful in carrying out Christ's teachings as they might have been, and as they would try to be, I am sure, if all the consequences were more generally known. We have learned that this education, when left for the afterlife, is too often complicated by the results of unkind deeds and thoughts in this life, and also by having to unlearn many things that have been wrongly learned or understood while here. This last is a handicap little thought of by those who have not investigated. It is frequently a serious one. It has been brought to our notice very strongly in various ways. The following is one instance:—

"I am not trying for marvels or wonders, but I do want to try to give a plain, simple statement of the life here, that may lead some anxious, fearing soul into more faith and happiness. I wish I could save them from looking forward with fear into the dark unknown.

Will you try to take what you can, and I will try and write what I can, of comforting thought to all those who are really trying to live the right life on earth, and desiring a new inspiration for the future.

"Many come into this life in such ignorance that they sink immediately into a long, long sleep; and they may lose years, sometimes many precious years, before coming into spirit consciousness. Tell all who come in the circle of your influence that they are making their future now, and can almost control this future condition, if they will only seek the truth and abide by it while still on earth.

"I do not often preach, but I feel like a sermon tonight. For the souls that come to this side come in such multitudes that they can scarcely be counted, yet *only here and there are the spiritually developed ones*—the ones who can enter into this life with joy and commence the development of spiritual power at once. The pity of it gets hold of us here now and then, and we feel like trying to bombard the earth with spirit bombs—something to make people think; something to force them away from their material thoughts, pleasures, and plans.

"We are obliged to begin our work with them as we would begin with children; and not even in that way when they first come. They sink into a state that is hard to be described. They are not even ready to think. Brain and sense and heart and soul have so long been educated wrongly that silence and unconsciousness are the only remedies at first. Then there comes a confused awakening, with all their human habits of thought and all their evil selfishness predominant. What can be done then except to put strong forces in control, that they at least may be kept from influencing others. You cannot conceive of this work, I am sure, but it is very real here."

'But you do not do this—you with all your dainty, fairy children to teach?'

"No, but I watch others in the patient, self-controlled effort, and I realize how strong must be their faith and hope to continue in the work. They do succeed at last, but it is often a long and weary way; and but for the strong, bright, and enduring faith of such workers and teachers, it would be almost unendurable."

'Such spirits are kept separate, are they not?'

"Yes, surely. Each 'goes to his own place,' as the Bible says. But we can watch the work of transformation and we can give to the workers our own best thoughts and encouragement. That is our part of it."

We said we had thought of this phase there and had spoken of it.

"It exists, and is one of the great opportunities for work for the great and blessed spirits who undertake it.

"I have preached a sermon this time; but it may be well for you to know of the darker shadows over here. But we are also blessed with the sight of the brave spirits who are working with the depraved ones, and we are also blessed with the knowledge that their work is not in vain. Of course all who come are not vicious; only unspiritual, living in the material thought. These are slow to come into the life of the spirit, but come far more rapidly than those whose evil natures have to be transformed.

"We were full of the subject, for we have been watching the work of some of our fine spirits with the low and debased ones of earth, and were filled with the pity of it—the unnecessary waste of lives there and the unnecessary waste of time here in bringing them into spirit lives. Then too, all these brave teachers who give themselves to this work might be released for other and pleasanter work, if only, if only, the earth people knew the truth."

It is difficult for the earth people to learn the truth. This phase of it has not been very prominent in most messages from the other side. Moreover, it is difficult to comprehend the full force of the truth when it does come to us. Notwithstanding our surprise on learning

152

of the slow progress that many make after leaving this life, even then we did not grasp its full meaning. And we are still startled at times as some new phase of undevelopment is brought to our attention.

At a much later date the following was also written on this subject:—

"We wish to tell you of our work among the circles of the undeveloped spirits. There are so many who have to be cared for, that it becomes a very great work; and as time passes, this has become very much systematized. Vast numbers are cared for, and when they begin to understand where they are, they are classified according to their temperament and ability, and put in the care of teachers who are best fitted for them.

"It is a wonderful sight to see the patience and judgment of these teachers. There is no lack of them, for they are recruited from the ranks of those whom they start on the upward path. So many are grateful for the help given them, that they in turn devote long periods of their life on this plane to aiding the unfortunates whose needs they know so well.

"When a spirit first arrives it is cared for much as patients are entered in a hospital. They are helpless, and often remain so for long periods. In this condition they are little care. When sensation and consciousness begin to show, they need attention. Many cannot be reached at all by their guides, as you know by those who have been brought to you. Sometimes they can be led from place to place, but that is all. Sometimes they need to be surrounded by guards to prevent them from running hither and thither without reason. When they can be made to realize that they still live and are in the spirit world, they can be easily managed. But the progress of each is according to the ability to receive and understand the teachings given them.

"We think we can truthfully say that one-fourth of those who come to this side are made to understand the needs of spirit life in a reasonable time. But the remaining three-fourths are our problem and care. We do not mean that all of this large number are unable to advance, but that they are slow, and sometimes very slow. We have many, many whom we seem unable to help at all. We do not know that it is impossible for them to advance, but we do know that many of them have made no advancement since we came; and we are told that some of them have been in this condition for centuries.

"It is pitiful. It seems to us unnecessary. It does not seem to be so much because of difference in ability, as from a state of mind brought about by forming wrong opinions and ideas when in earth life. And the position they occupied in that life seems not to have much to do with it. This makes us think that it is unnecessary, and we wish some way could be found that would make the world understand what is needed.

"With all our writing we wonder if we have conveyed a true impression of how important this work is with us. There are so many that great numbers of our most valued friends and neighbors here are required to devote nearly all their time to caring for and teaching them. We wish the truth of spirit communication could be accepted more generally there. Then we could the more convincingly tell of what our life consists, and of what is necessary there to enable the spirit to at once enter into the joys of this existence. We feel that at present it is placing an unnecessary burden on us here, and holding back the advancement, in a way, of multitudes of our finest souls."

A specific instance of the slow progress that can occur is given below, and it is a pleasure to think that we probably assisted a little in his enlightenment. In the succeeding pages are further instances showing conditions so astounding that they will seem almost unbelievable to one newly introduced to the subject.

This first instance concerns a friend of Sis's, one whom she knew very well in earlier days. I will call him Frank Chase. He was a man of high ideals concerning this life, but very positive in his beliefs. He held in ridicule all ideas of communication with the unseen world, if indeed he held a belief that there was such a world. His interest was most keen in the mechanics and scientific discoveries of the day. He passed over in early manhood.

Sis had inquired about him several times, but received little information beyond the statement that he had not advanced very far, which she thought very surprising. Finally, when writing, we were asked quite unexpectedly:—

"Will you send a message to Frank Chase? If you did he might like to come to this circle. If we can interest him in this work it will be well for him.

"He seems to question everything, and doubts even the spiritual life. He knows, of course, that he has passed away from earth, but is busy explaining that and many other things with a philosophy of his own. He has a bright brain, and we wish to turn it to the truth and lead him into the right thought here. That is why I asked you to send him a message. He does not know you are communicating. We believe that if he can find himself—that is, realize that he is a spirit and living a spirit life already—that he will begin to study and grow."

The next day the pencil wrote:—

"After talking with you yesterday I turned, and with the quickness of thought, was far away—so far that it would have taken you days to accomplish the journey. We went to see the one to whom we wish you to speak, and we have brought him to our circle to talk to you. He does not believe it can be done. Can you convince him? Will you speak to him?"

Sis said:—

'Well, Frank Chase, are you really here to talk to me again after all these years?'

Mary said:—

"He does not believe it is you. Call to his mind something he used to know."

Sis complied by asking:—

'Do you remember going to New York to see a young lady?'
"Will you tell him how she looked?"

Sis gave a short description of the young lady, and Mary said:—

"Will you keep on. He is impressed."

Sis asked if he remembered this young lady coming to where he lived.

"Keep right on. He is interested."

After further talk we were told:—

"He knows now it is you, and is overjoyed to know it is possible to talk with and hear from earth, which he has never done before."

After some further conversation, Mary said:—

"He is so surprised that he can hardly credit it at all. Yet he knows that only you could tell him some of these things. We will bring him again soon: it is a good beginning. He is startled, and can hardly believe; but will probably wish to investigate, as that is his turn of mind, and that is what we wish."

We asked if they could explain how he had been getting along all these years without learning more.

"Try to think of yourself in a dream—a long dream—and everything happening in ways that are strange, yet you do not wonder about it. Your dream accepts the things as true. That is as near as I can describe his situation. When he first came he was met by his father

156

and sister, but they failed to reach his reasoning mind and he has wandered on in this condition through all these years."

At another time he came of his own accord to Mary, wishing to talk. After a short conversation Sis asked if in all that time he had been there he had heard of the many wonderful inventions that had appeared here in the meantime. He had not, and wished to know about them. First was the telegraph. Yes, he remembered that. But the telephone was new, and the wireless and the automobile. Then we went on to tell of the great war, the immense ships that carried our soldiers, and the terrible guns. He had heard a little of the war, but did not believe it possible to do such things.

"What are the good things of earth?" he asked.

This came near being a 'poser,' but Sis spoke of the Red Cross work, the hospitals, the aid to the starving, etc. Mary said:—

"He thinks the world must be in a terrible condition with so much science producing evil things. Tell him of the great vessel that was sunk by the Germans. Tell him about the ship that was sunk by an iceberg."

We talked some time, and after some remark of Sis's, he said:—

"What am I going to hear from you next! No one else could have told me the things you have. I did not know it could be done."

Mary added:—

"He is dazed with the thought, but he will take it to think over as he did last time. You are certainly getting hold of him and we must keep it up."

'This is startling, Mary! How can such things be?'

"Will you believe that each one makes his own life; each one has the chance and must develop accordingly. Frank Chase's condition was caused by too much doubt, too much unbelief in a spirit life. He would not believe he was in a heavenly sphere and would not believe that he needed help, but argued himself into a strange and persistent unbelief until the desire for anything different almost disappeared."

The next time he came Mary wrote for him as follows:—

"I am here. Your teacher will write for me. I have been so unbelieving that I could get nothing, of course; and so I had no proof of the connection between the two worlds. But what you have said convinced me, and I am studying now so that I too can get in touch with mortal lives."

Mary added:—

"There have been years, he says, when he believed he was on some plane above the earth, but he did not understand that this plane might be the beginning of heavenly life for him. It is hard to make you understand, and he says now it is hard for him to understand; and it seems to him more like a long, long dream than anything else he can compare it to. He is learning fast and is far happier than before and pursues his studies eagerly."

This was an amazing experience for us. We had read something of such things, but it was all so strange we had passed it by. But this brought the truth to our realization with much force. Many have been brought to us in later months, and we understand there are other circles also engaged in this work. It seems that these unfortunate spirits can frequently be helped from this side, even when the guardians there can make no impression whatever. Most of them eventually find their way out of the fog in some manner, although there has been a hint that it is possible to be almost indefinitely delayed. It is certain that many remain for years and years before they grasp the meaning of the spirit life.

Such spirits have not necessarily led evil lives while here. More often this spiritual handicap is the result of too strong a belief in some superstition, some creed, or some philosophy on earth; a case of being certain that one way is right and all others wrong. Such beliefs and philosophies continue with them more or less strongly on the other side, just as superstitions sometimes cling to one here in spite of all the evidence there may be to show they are without foundation.

That the attainment of a development complete enough to enable one to advance to higher planes may be delayed almost indefinitely is revealed by an incident which I will quote just as it appears on our records:—

In looking over our records there will be found a number of instances when Mary has said that Sis was surrounded by a cloud. Several times she has said she thought this cloud was the result of some other power trying to manifest through her pencil. In these cases very little has been written; and numerous times when Sis has been alone not a movement occurred.

This was the case this afternoon. A little later, when I was present, only a few words came through. Late this afternoon, however, Sis tried to get passive when alone and her hand began to shake, showing that someone wished to write. Mary then wrote freely and gave an explanation of the perplexing troubles.

Sis was trying to get in communication with Mary because of a letter I had received from a friend. It seems that this friend had been to a psychic who had given a message for Sis. This message was as follows:—

"There is an ancient spirit, way back in the times of Mahomet, who says he has been trying to reach Miss D., and says he has something of importance to say to her, and begs you to give a message which he wants to send. He wants her to write as a heading on her paper, 'The Seers and Sages of the Present Day,' and then wait in silence for his message."

When Mary finally succeeded in writing, the following was received:—

"We are here, and you were led by us. Do not doubt. We could not give that other one the opportunity. He would have misguided you."

'Was it the 'ancient spirit' we were told to expect?'

"Yes, he is an ancient force or teacher, but is not the kind we trust. He has not learned the real truth in all the ages he has lived. He would teach you of occult mysteries as they existed in the olden time. We do not wish the unseen to be represented by mysteries, rites, and observances. Remember that we belong to an age in which the teachings of Christ have purified religious belief; and we in the unseen strive to make His teachings still powerful on earth. We do not know just what that other message would have been, but we do know that you, as well as we, wish for the truth as Christ gave it to the world. Are you satisfied?"

'Yes, that is what we wish.'

"We try to guard you always from such influences, and it is because we do this that at times you do not even get us. We cannot come through an influence so strong that it takes all our force to neutralize it.

"You trust us and that is well. Keep with us as long as we teach the truth that Christ taught on earth; humility, unselfishness, the love of humanity, and the striving to make the world better."

Sis inquired of the reliability of any of the ancient sages or rulers who wrote through others.

"We do not know any of the ancient kings or princes. We cannot describe or even see them. But this teacher who wished to control your pencil has been here before and we have checked his influence; and as he said, he could not get a message to you. Are you sorry?"

'No. We wish your guidance and protection.'

"You are safe while you keep that attitude. The world is likely to go astray if led by those who teach strange rites and occult practices of long ago. Christ and the truth as made known by Christ are what we wish to bring to the world. You are safe in such truth and such teaching."

'Was it because you were trying to prevent other powers from sending messages, that I so many times have been unable to write?'

"Yes. We often have all our power taken in simply neutralizing other influences. Remember that only mind or spirit force can be used, and if used in preventing other influences, it cannot at the same time be used in giving out messages."

'Why did you not tell me what the trouble was at the time?'

"We do not like to admit the power at the time. Be satisfied. We are protecting you always. Goodbye now."

Soon after this I came in, and after hearing what had been written, I said:—

'Well, Mary, we are very grateful to you for guarding the writing.'

"You may well be, for it means your protection and your determination to receive only the truth."

Then to Sis:—

"Do you see why we wish you to be our medium, even if you have less psychic power than some others?"

I said it was astonishing how many were slow in developing, and how long they were in seeing the truth.

"Can you see how very long people or spirits may be fascinated with their own beliefs? They are so unwilling to be convinced! No wonder that Christ taught the people that they must become as little children.

"We can tell you that many times we have neutralized powerful forces that were untruthful and malicious. We are constantly on guard lest some unworthy power succeeds in getting a message to you. We believe you would recognize it usually, but some spirits are subtle, and give sophistries in language that would conceal the malicious influence."

'Mary, just why has nothing been said of this before? Were you afraid we would not understand?'

"Mary does not like to speak of the evil here ordinarily. It unsettles some earthly minds in their previous beliefs of a heavenly perfection, and we prefer to use constructive rather than destructive influence."

STORIES OF UNDEVELOPED SPIRITS

Somewhere in our records is the statement, "The way is long and the road a weary one for those who have not learned their lessons on earth." In later months this truth has been especially emphasized through both Sis's pencil and my own. Many stories of the difficulties encountered, and of the time wasted in overcoming them, have been related by various souls who have been brought to us. Little do most people here realize the conditions that will confront them as they enter the spirit world: the time that will be wasted by most because they are so material-minded as to be unimpressed by spirit influence; the bewilderment that will cloud the path of many because they have no understanding of the use of spirit faculties, and so are hindered in their advancement by the dazed and incorrect impressions of sight and hearing; the miseries that will be the lot of some because of fixed but erroneous ideas of what heaven is like, which may cause them to wander long in darkness; while the number who cannot realize that they have even left the earth life at all is so great as to be appalling to one who is ignorant of conditions on the other side. Only a few, it seems, are at all prepared to understand what the life there means, and only the occasional one enters quickly into the joys of the spirit world.

As the reader may learn in our previous volume, *Spirit World and Spirit Life*, no one passes into spirit life "with consciousness at every moment of the change." Most are unconscious for some time, partly because of weakened vitality from sickness, but frequently from inability to use spirit perceptions. This period of unconsciousness varies from a few hours or a few days for the most fortunate, up to weeks and months and even years for one who may be selfish and materialistic. And after the awakening—what?

In the following pages we will let some who have passed through these experiences tell their own stories. If the perusal of these statements, and of others that follow, does not suggest to the reader the importance of acquiring a knowledge in this life of some of the requirements for spiritual advancement, this book is failing in its mission. Not that it is claimed that all should try to become spiritualistic mediums, or spiritualists, or even attend séances. But it is insisted that all should familiarize themselves with two facts: that there is a future life, and that they will have to perceive and understand this future life by other than their present material senses. For, strangely, this knowledge seems to be possessed by an almost unbelievably small number. Added to these two facts is a third one that ordinarily should need no emphasis; it should be self-evident. This is that right living, a life of unselfishness, is necessary for spiritual advancement both in the mortal and in the spirit life.

We have been so impressed with the importance of this phase of the subject that I am including at considerable length quite a number of illustrations. Where names are given, I have for several reasons used other than the correct ones, and in some places the matter has been condensed.

We have sometimes used the Ouija board a few minutes before Sis began any automatic writing, as it seemed an aid in inducing passivity. One evening our friends seemed to have been waiting for us, for the little triangle began to move at once, spelling out the question:—

"Who moves this?"
'Is it not Mary?'

"No."

'Who is it?'

"Fourth cousin from David Fuller."

This sounded like an attempt at being facetious, but I replied:—

'I don't remember any David Fuller.'

But the name called to my mind the marriage of a relative when I was a small boy, and I added:—

'I knew a David Walker who married a Fuller?'
"Yes."
'Are you he?'
"Yes."
'Dr. Walker?'
"I am Dr. Walker."
'Well, this is a surprise.'

I was much puzzled. My father and Dr. Walker had both passed over more than twenty years before. I asked if he had seen my father.

"I hardly get any news."

I began to have a suspicion that he did not realize where he was or what had happened to him. But I hesitated to say anything that would indicate that I thought this, for I also feared that it might be a sort of joke that was being tried on us by some malicious spirit. I asked:—

'Where are you?'

"I am in a place I do not know."

Sis took the pencil here, and Mary wrote:—

164

"He has not developed far, for he was not advanced when he came to this side. He is not a stranger to us, though we have only now learned his acquaintance with you. He hardly realizes that he has passed over. He knows he is not at his home on earth, and he wonders about his conditions here. He was not a bad man, just indifferent toward all spiritual things, and thought that death ended all. He would have liked to have you place him—tell him where he is and how he came here. For he is in the condition of one who has partly lost his mind: the earthly brain gone and the spirit force not yet in control."

'I got the impression that he does not really know he has passed into another world.'

"No. He is really in a pitiful state, and we wish to bring him out of it. We think you can help."

'Tell me what to do.'

"When he comes again try to tell something about his earlier life, something that will strengthen his memory of the past. Through that memory we may bring him to realize his sickness and his death and his coming into this life."

We had heard of cases somewhat like this, and we talked this one over at the time. But it had mostly dropped from our minds when some two weeks later it was brought to the fore again in a way that made a great impression on us. The record makes strange reading. But all thought of him was far removed when we took up Ouija.

"We are wishing to tell you of a man who wishes to write."

After some difficulty they managed to partially spell the name Walker, and I asked if he were there.

"Yes."

I said to him:—

'You have been away from home some time. Do you remember being sick?'

"Yes."

'Do you know what happened?'

"I do not remember."

'What happens when people do not get well? You have had such cases in your practice.'

"They died."

'Had you thought that your sickness might have ended that way?'

"That is not true."

'What makes you think it is not true?'

"I am alive."

'Yes, but you are living under different conditions, are you not?'

"Rather."

'If you believe that you are alive, try to comprehend that there is a great future before you. That will help you to move forward into better conditions.'

"That is a new idea."

Then after a short wait he asked:—

"Am I dead?"

'Yes—what you think of as dead; that is, your body is dead.'

He seemed to ponder over this a little, then asked again:—

"I am asking if I am dead?"

'Do you not think it might be true? Are you not different from what you were?'

"I am surprised."

'Have you not wondered where you were?'

"I did not know. Can you tell me where I am?"

'In the spirit world; a certain portion of it, at least. You will see more of it after awhile.'

Again there was a little wait; then:—

"Are *you* dead?"

'No, I am still on earth. Can you tell us what your surroundings are like where you are now?'

"Something like the earth.'

'Do you not move faster?'

"No."

'Perhaps you have not yet learned?'

"I have learned nothing."

'Do you see others about you?'

"Yes."

'If you will tell them what you want I am sure they will help you.'

"How shall I talk to them?"

'I hardly know how to tell you. Perhaps if you think strongly what you wish, you will understand their reply.'

"Are *they* dead?"

'Yes, and they wish to help you.'

"I am not sure I am dead."

I explained that I could not see him.

"No. That cannot be true."

'Can you see me?'

"Yes. I see you as a shadow."

'Do I look as people did on earth?'

"No."

'That is because you have left the earth.'

"Are you sure?"

'Yes, quite sure. Do you see a beautiful lady near you?'

"Yes."

"Well, she will help you to understand about the things that puzzle you."

"No. I am not dead!"

'Mary, what shall I say to him. I am at my wits—'

"I hardly know myself, but he will understand soon."

'It seems almost unbelievable. We are told that 'each goes to his own place.' But he seems to have no place?'

"No, not a place."

'It is so strange. Does it seem so to you, or do you have many such?'

"We see many, but the pity of it grows."

'Where were his spirit guardians?'

"He would not listen; his own preconceived ideas were too strong. His spirit friends were powerless; just as we are powerless, oftentimes, to send warning or blessing to the earth friends we love so well."

'But he has not been on earth for a long time?'

"Just the same; his mortal beliefs were stronger than any influence from here."

He was not brought to us again, but we have been told that he was much impressed by the experience. He had accepted the fact that he was in the spirit world, and was slowly acquiring his spirit powers.

At another time the pencil wrote:—

"We have many who need help, and we will bring some of them to you if you are willing to try."

'We will gladly do what we can.'

Apparently two earthbound souls were brought at once, for the pencil soon wrote:—

"We are here. What can you tell us? We are two poor humans who are confined in darkness and distress. Can you help us?"

'How long have you been there?'

"I forget. It is all a blank."

'How did you come to the place where you are?'

"We do not know. We found ourselves here and do not know who brought us."

'Is it at all like the earth?'

"No, we never saw anything so unlovely."

'Has it occurred to you that you have left the earth?'

168

"No, we have never left the earth, but we do not know where we are."

'Has anyone ever told you that you have left the earth, and are what the world calls dead?'

"No, not anyone that we believed."

'It is true, nevertheless, and you are now in the spirit world.'

"No, we are not there. The spirit world is bright and this is dark."

'It seems dark to you because you have not developed your spirit sight. You must study for that.'

"Who could teach us?"

'Some of those about you.'

"No, we can see as well as they."

'What do you remember of your earth life?'

"We had a home, children, friends. Here we have no one."

'Why did you leave your home and children?'

"We did not leave. We awoke and found ourselves here."

'What put you to sleep?'

'I am trying to tell you that you have passed through the sleep called death, and are in the spirit life.'

"What are you telling us? That cannot be!"

'Would you like to have your sight cleared so that you can understand?'

"Yes, if true."

'We know that you can come into spirit sight.'

"We will try. What shall we do?"

'We think Mary can help you.'

"Mary? Where is she?"

We asked Mary if she was there.

"Yes, and near them, but they cannot see us."

'Can they hear you?'

"We will try."

After a moment she wrote:—

"Mary thinks they hear a little."

Then we asked the unfortunates:—

'Did you hear a sound?'

"Yes, a little. Who was it?"

'That was Mary. I am sure you can learn to hear if you will try.'

"We will try. Tell us how."

Listen now. Mary will try again. Did you hear this time?'

"A little. I believe you tell the truth."

"Not at all."

'You can learn.'

"We don't know. How do you know?"

'Is there anyone near you?'

"There is a shadowy form. What is it?"

"We will try anything to get out of this."

'Listen again.'

"We hear a faint musical sound. Is that our hearing coming to us?"

'I am sure it is.'

"We heard a word then. It was 'love.' Was that right?"

'Mary, did they hear aright?'

"Yes, love was the word."

We then asked the others:—

'Now do you believe you can get the rest?'

"We believe we can. And it is the first ray of light and hope that has penetrated this darkness. We will come again if we can find you."

'We will ask Mary to bring you.'

"Will she? We will come if she will help."

We asked if Dee had been present.

"Yes, and listening and watching. It is wonderful how these earthbound souls need friends. With all our love and all our endeavor we have been unable to pierce the darkness of their still earthly perceptions."

'Do you know anything about these two?'

"We think they have been here some months, perhaps years. We have no means of knowing as they have no perception of time. They were brought to us by another circle."

The next one proved to be an old-time acquaintance of Sis's.

"There is one you have known who has come to us for help. He is not sure of himself, hardly knows himself as spirit, yet feels the difference from mortal life. What can you say to him?"

'You say it is someone I have known?'

"Yes, and someone whom you can influence."

'Has he lately passed over?'

"Not long since, but he feels himself unable to progress without help. He never thought of life here in the way he finds it, and does not know how to adapt himself to conditions."

'Can you tell me his earth name?'

"No, but he came from a place that you lived in for awhile, not your home town."

'Can he talk to me?'

"We will try. He says you were more advanced than he, and he thought you in the wrong, and now he wonders if you were right. He believed in the creed of the church—heaven, hell, day of judgment, golden streets or their similarity—and has not found these things here, and he wonders if this can be heaven after all."

'Does he not find it more beautiful?'

"In a way; but not so symbolical, perhaps; not so unreal to mortal thought. Tell him what you have learned of spirit life. He can hear you, we think, but we can only tell by his replies. He says he learned to sing under your training."

Sis mentioned several places, and after one of them she was told:—

"Yes, that is it."

'Could he tell me his name?'

I took the pencil, because at times I could get them better than Sis. This time I did not succeed very well. My pencil wrote a name that suggested that of an old acquaintance, although there was only one syllable right. The name suggested proved to be correct.

171

She asked him:—

'Can you hear Mary?'

"A little, but not as well as you."

'You are still held by your old earthly ideas and sensations, it seems. You have not gained your spirit powers.'

"Well, that is it, then? And it makes it seem as if I were in a strange country and without a guide."

'How much can you see?'

"Not a great deal. But it looks more like the earth than like the heaven I always imagined."

'You will find as you advance in your spirit powers that you will see much beauty.'

"They tell me so, but how do you know?"

'I have always had that idea, and from what we are told, it seems that I was right. Did you like to study while here?'

"Not much. I was dull, I am afraid."

'You will find by study that heaven is very beautiful.'

'Was the earth as fine as you would have liked?'

"No."

'Was your home and surroundings all you could imagine?'

"No."

'Well, by study you will learn that you can have everything as fine as you wish. Is not that worth working for?'

"Yes, of course."

'You have heard of the 'many mansions' in heaven?'

"Yes, but I never dreamed of their being real. Mary brings me to you to learn of the place I am in! How strange! It seems as if I ought to be telling you!"

'You will know all about it if you will study.'

"How shall I begin?"

'It is a little hard to tell you, but you must first learn to use your spirit sight and hearing.'

"But how can I learn?"

'Can you hear Mary?'

"Yes, a little... Yes, I heard her. She asked me if I could see her. I could see a shadow and the shadow spoke!"

Then apparently Mary spoke to him again.

"Yes, she says I can learn both to hear and to see. Do you think so?"

This was written with much excitement. We assured him it was true.

"Well, I will surely try. Is this my first lesson?"

Mary thinks he will develop fast now.

"Well, I heard more clearly then, and begin to think you are right. When are you *coming here*?"

After he had gone we asked Mary how it was that he could hear us and not hear her.

"That is because he is still in the mortal vibrations, and memories of earth life are more powerful than the unused spirit faculties."

Again one was brought who claimed to know Sis, but she never learned his name.

"There is one here who says he knew you long ago. He is troubled and doubting his own identity, and we have brought him here to you."

'Can he hear?'"
"Yes; your voice better than ours. Ask him a question."
'Do you know where you lived?'
"No, I forgot. I was very sick and they moved me to this place when I was asleep."
'Can you see anyone around you?'
"Not well. I must have lost my eyesight when sick."
'Do you remember what happened when you were sick?'

"No, except medicine, doctors, nurses, and now and then friends see me."

'Do you know where I lived?'

"Yes, you lived in a place not far from where I was. I was not at home, I remember that now."

'Are you John Romley?'

"No. I knew him though."

'Did you know he is near you?'

"No. Is he here?"

'He was ill and died in a hospital.'

"No, he is alive, for I have seen him."

'Perhaps, but John has passed through that which we call death. I suspect you have done the same, and do not realize that instead of dying, you are still alive.'

"No, I don't see how that can be. This is not heaven, and it isn't hell; and there are no other places for the soul to go."

'If with your eyes bandaged someone had led you to another place, would you have believed all was light when you thought it night?'

"No. But I would have torn the bandage off."

'You are now blinded by the bandages of your earthly memories and do not know of the light about you yet.'

"What do you mean?"

'I mean that you should tear off those earthly bandages and learn to use your new senses.'

"My senses? What are they?"

'Spirit sight and spirit hearing. Have you these?'

"Not much of either. I am nearly blind and deaf. What can I do?"

'Are you willing to try to learn?'

"Yes. Tell me what to do."

'We have a good friend there whose name is Mary. She is near you. Can you see her?'

'Can you hear her?'

"No, I think not."

'She brought you to me.'

"Mary? Who is she?"

'Mary, can you speak to him?'

'Did you hear anything?'

"Nothing but a whisper without any words."

'Well, that is a beginning. Try again.'

"Yes, I heard a little sound then."

'Keep listening and you will soon hear.'

"Is that true, that I am to listen and hear?"

'Yes, you will soon learn and will acquire wonderful powers.'

"Yes! Yes! I hope that is true! Help me! Help me! if you can!"

'Listen again.'

"I heard her. She said I was in heaven. Is that true?"

'You are in a part of heaven that is near earth.'

"That is true, you think?"

'I am sure of it.'

"Ask Mary, as you call her, to try again. I believe I can learn to hear."

'Mary, did you hear what he said?'

"Yes, I will ask his name."

"She asks my name! I can't find it! What shall I do?"

'Don't worry. You will soon find it.'

"Will she stay with me and help me?"

'Mary, what shall I tell him?'

"Tell him I or some other friend will be with him every minute until he becomes conscious of his own life and his own spirit powers."

This was repeated to him.

"Well I am so glad. I cannot tell you how glad! It is like waking from a nightmare."

'Mary, what happened to him?'

"We have not heard his life history, but we think it is only a case of indifference toward all things spiritual, and possibly a little contempt for the weakness of so-called Christians in spending so much time in 'preaching and praying and psalm-singing.'"

Still another one who had known Sis was brought to us.

"We wish to have you take a few words from someone here. We will write for him. He says he knew you long ago when you were in another town."

Sis finally guessed the place.

"Yes, that is the one. We think your teacher is here and remembers you. He says you studied with him."

'Well, well! It seems strange that he should remember me?'

"His memory is very clear. He died apparently in good health in the midst of plans for the future. He had never given much thought to this life and the change was difficult for him to make. He was rebellious at first and unhappy. But his guides were patient and have brought him into an understanding of this life. He was not unconscious long, and awakened to find his past had slipped away from him, and his future a shadowy unknown. We have many such; but his mind—his mortal mind—was so vigorous that he could the less easily comprehend a condition in which the mortal mind was of no avail. He commenced as a little child might do, and has had a long time in initiation. But he has come into the light at last."

'If the mortal mind failed, I should think the memory would go too?'

"No, not necessarily. The memory is a spirit power and is usually more keen in this life than in the other."

'What is his occupation?'

"He has not been here in his spirit perception long enough to be brought into that for which he will be most fitted, but he gravitates toward music, and we think that will enter largely into his work."

'How did he come to know you and to remember me?'

"We are communicating with mortals, and that was his great desire. He has been in the circle repeatedly, and at last recognized you as a former pupil."

'Is there anything he wishes to say?'

"Not much, we think, because he does not yet fully grasp

conditions here. But he was much pleased to know of someone who was sending words across what to him is the shadowland of death. He will become more and more satisfied with this life and will be happy beyond his present power of belief. Have you a word to say to him?"

'Tell him I am longing for the happiness there.'

"We have told him and he is surprised. He cannot understand that attitude, for the earth life still weaves a strong attraction about him."

'I remember him as one who might have had much human pleasure.'

"We think that is true. And his lack of comprehension—his lack of looking forward to this life while on earth—is a hindrance now. But he has made a great advance from his first dismal impressions, and will surely come into the light before long."

Among the many who have been brought to us was one who, we were told, went to that side far back in the last century. I seemed to get the impression of 1840 or 1850. Mary said:—

"He wishes to know how many people there are in the United States now?"

'There are about 110,000,000 now. I suppose they scarcely numbered 40,000,000 then—possibly less?'

"He says he thinks that was about the number. Will you tell him what has happened to the city of Morningside?"

'Morningside?'

"Yes."

'Near New York City?'

"Yes."

'It was out from the city some ways then, was it not?'

"Yes, it was some distance from New York."

'Well, New York has some seven million people now, and extends miles beyond Morningside, and crowded with immense apartment houses nearly all the way.'

"What must life be like!"

I described the subway jam of late afternoons.

"Well, life has not improved in some ways, it seems to me. We thought New York a great city. Some of us thought it too big. What must it be now! I remember that most of the business was down toward the Battery."

'Was Fifth Avenue prominent then?'

"Yes, Fifth Avenue was the street of fashion."

'Do you remember how far it extended?'

"Not exactly, but not very far. It seems to me that the streets numbered up to fifty or sixty. Morningside was a town where some of the merchants resided, and I was one of the number. I conducted a business on Broadway, just a small business, but it seemed very important to me then. We went to our business by carriage, and only in the last few years of my life were there streetcars."

'Not out to Morningside?'

"No, just in the main part of the city of New York."

I spoke further of the terrible congestion.

"Perhaps it is as well that I have no need to be there."

'So heaven is not crowded like that?'

"I haven't found it so yet."

'You are still on the lower plane?'

"Yes, I am trying to find out what there is for me to do here. It is only a short time since I realized that I had died. I was not unconscious for very long, but all these years I have been trying to find out why I could not locate my people and my friends. It seems now like a dream, but as I passed through it it was very real, and I suffered loneliness and despair all that time."

'Have you any idea why you were in that condition so long?'

"I never gave a thought to the future life while I was on earth. I don't know that I denied such an existence, but it gave me no concern. My life was filled with the affairs of the moment. I was in comfortable circumstances and had no especial cares. When I ceased the mortal existence I had nothing to take its place. I could not understand what had happened. I seemed to be lost, and could find no one to help me. I know now of course that many were trying to help me, but none of their influence could penetrate the shell of material thought that still confined me."

'I wish people could understand that condition and its cause.'

"Yes, do spread the knowledge that you are acquiring. If you can be the means of helping one soul to avoid the agony and terror through which I passed your efforts will be well worth while."

'When you were on earth what did you think when a friend passed away?'

"I don't believe I thought at all."

'Did you have a family?'

"Yes, and most of them are here. Some of them have been awaiting my recovery for many years. Some of them are passing through experiences more or less similar to mine."

'What did you do all these years?'

"I hardly know now how I did occupy my time. I realize now that only a part of me was alive, only a very small part. But that part seemed to feel the awful terrors and agonies as much or even more than any complete earthly personality could do."

'Can you tell us more about it so we can tell others?'

"I ought to be able to do so, for even now the memories are terrible. I seemed to be in an unknown country, alone, and at all times filled with a terror that dangers lurked all about me. What these dangers were I could not have told. But I seemed striving all the time to escape them, and yet knew no place to go. I felt that everyone had deserted me. I was filled with hate that they could so treat me. Any thought aside from those of fear was mostly one of some plan of revenge on those whom I believed must be responsible for my situation. It was a long nightmare of dread and hate. I don't think a material body could have long survived such tortures.

"After what seemed ages, I began to hear something like musical sounds, and these began to have a quieting effect. Later I began to sense that there were other beings about me. And eventually I acquired my spirit powers, and am now beginning to understand some of the great glories of the life here that I have been so long in comprehending.

"Do spread the word. Make people understand what even mere apathy concerning the future may cause.

"Thank you for this opportunity to write."

The above writer says he realizes now that only a part of him was alive. Undoubtedly this is true. Nearly all such cases evidence a dazed and bewildered condition in which the powers of reasoning are so deadened as to be almost lost. When they are brought to us the influence from an earthly personality seems to release their spirit powers in some way. It could almost be said that the doors of the prison in which they have been confined were thrown open by touching a spring that only an influence from earth could reach.

The two incidents following illustrate this vividly:—

"We have here in the circle a man who has had much trouble in realizing that he has left the earth life. He was a thinker on religious subjects, but had reasoned things out according to his own satisfaction, and now cannot find conditions that correspond to his conclusions, and he cannot understand what has happened. He can both see and hear a little, but he thinks he is still among earth people, and among those who scoff at his ideas. So he will not listen to them. He has a few friends who have formed somewhat similar opinions, and they feel that they are a little party of apostles who are persecuted by infidels, or something like that. They do not realize that they do not have their physical bodies and material brains."

'Can we talk with them?'

"We wish you would try. We think he will listen to you because no one has spoken to them from earth, and it may be that an 'earth spirit' can have more influence than we. We will bring him to you."

180

Then after a moment:—

"We have told him that a friend wishes to talk with him."

I said to him that I understood that he felt that he was lost.

"Yes. I do not understand what has happened. I have missed my old friends for some time, and I do not know where I am. I was ill and fell asleep and must have wandered away from home."

'Do you know how long you were ill?'

"No. It seems to me a long time, but I do not remember. I thought I was very ill."

'Had you thought that your illness might have led to death, and that your falling asleep was the passing?'

"No, I had not thought of that. I wonder if that can be true?"

'I think it is.'

"Well, I cannot understand it. I thought the life of the spirit was one of happiness and glory, but I have found nothing like that."

'I think if you will cultivate your powers of sight and hearing you will find some of the happiness and glory.'

"I wonder! You have given me an idea! I am alone here now, but have several companions part of the time."

'Can you see anyone about you now?'

"Yes, there seem to be other beings of some kind."

'Listen carefully and see if you cannot hear one of them talk to you.'

There was a slight pause.

"Yes, one of them has just spoken, and he says you are telling me the truth."

'Yes, I am sure I am telling you the truth.'

"Well, well! I wonder if that can be! You have given me the first understanding I have had of what might be the explanation of my plight. I had felt all the time that I had somehow wandered into a strange country and among unfriendly people. I could make no one understand what had happened to me, or where my home was. I did find a few who seemed to be lost in the same way, and we have tried to comfort each other, and have been waiting and searching for something that would give us some clue to what had happened."

Then Mary wrote:—

"We think he will listen to us now, and if he does we can of course soon explain it all. We think just that hint was all that was necessary. We have tried to tell them these same things, but our influence seemed unavailing. It seems to be that the vibrations from one on earth are more penetrating—have a more convincing quality somehow. There may be an accurate explanation, but we have not learned just what it is. Some of the others you found more difficulty in impressing. This time, for some reason, it seemed very easy. Possibly just a difference in personality."

And now to close this chapter:—

"We will bring one to you who is not yet conscious that he has died. He thinks he is lost and wishes to find the way. We will write for him."

"I have been sick and wandered away. Why don't my friends find me?"

'Were you sick at your own home?'

"No, I was ill in a hospital, but I am not there now. I must have lost my mind and wandered away."

'Were you not too ill to walk?'

"I knew I was, but here I am, wandering about without either doctor or nurse. I must get back to the hospital again!"

'Do you know what happened?'

"What did happen?"

'Were you not growing weaker and weaker every day?'

"Yes. I remember the weakness, but now I have strength to walk! I must be better!"

'You have strength because you have left that old weak body, and are now spirit with spirit strength.'

"That cannot be! Oh, that cannot be! I left my friends, my business, my home. I must go back. Which way shall I go?"

'You cannot go back to your mortal body, but you can develop a wonderful life there.'

Mary interposed with:—

"We are trying to have him listen, but he persists that he must get back to his business and to his home."

'Did you have a wife?'

"No."

'A mother?'

"Yes. She is worrying about me. I must go to her."

'She does not worry now, for she knows that you have died and are beyond all earthly worries.'

"That cannot be true! Where am I?"

'You are in spirit land and need no longer worry over earthly cares and troubles.'

"Must I forget my mother and my business?"

'Forget your business but remember your mother. Can you see?'

"Not much."

'Can you hear?'

"I hear you."

'Can you see someone hear you?'

"No, I can only see a shadow."

Mary wrote in reply:—

"He cannot hear me yet."

'Try to listen.'

"I do not understand."

'Mary is near you trying to help.'

"Who is she?"

'A spirit like yourself. Listen and try to hear what she says.'

"I hear a faint sound. Is that Mary?"

'Yes. There are others near you, all trying to help."

"I am beginning to hear a little. They say I can soon hear and soon see and soon know there is joy in this life."

Then very slowly the pencil wrote:—

"I suppose it must be true."

Mary added:—

"We can take care of him now. When the earthborn spirit can hear and see, no matter how dimly, the worst is over. We can quickly teach him the rest."

FURTHER ACCOUNTS OF UNDEVELOPED SPIRITS

If the reader has carefully followed these stories so far, he will undoubtedly be struck with the variety of personalities presented; and this characteristic is still further displayed in those that follow. Ignorance of spiritual values, carelessness in any thought of a future life, selfishness of character, and a lack of knowledge concerning certain necessary requirements in the spirit world, especially those of sight and hearing—these are shared by most of those who are brought to us. But in other ways they are as different as such persons would naturally be in earth life, for personality always persists. If it did not, there would be no way of establishing the identity of anyone. In fact, no one would likely have any separate identity or individuality.

The critic will naturally note the similarity of the conditions in which the unfortunate spirits find themselves—the darkness, the silence, and their sense of being lost—and will at once jump to the conclusion that they all originated in the minds of those who received them. But I venture the assertion that if this critic arrives on the other side, with his mind hypnotized by his own unceasing suggestions that there is no future life, with no thought of the conditions that the lack of a material body necessitate, with no education of the spirit senses of sight and hearing, with a dazed and half-way dream-like mentality that does not reason out the meaning of the few ideas and sensations of which he is conscious—I say, he would certainly make just such remarks and ask just such questions, when he was first approached by one whose voice he could hear.

No! These stories did not originate in the subconscious mind of anyone. They are genuine accounts of unfortunate souls who have failed to understand the great change. And the sooner people can be induced to believe the truths that they imply, the sooner there will be a change in the general attitude toward a future life. And I think it is generally conceded that if a knowledge and realization of the facts of personal survival and of the need for preparation here were more nearly universal, the world would be a far better place than it is at present.

The reader may not care to go through all these stories, but if the doubter will read and analyze them carefully, he will find much food for thought. They are given for instruction, not for entertainment.

THE BUSINESSMAN

"We are bringing to you for help a man whose very soul was in his business and in money-making when on earth. We will write for him. He is not advanced at all, just keeps crying, 'Why am I here? Oh, why am I here?'"

We spoke to him but received no reply. Mary wrote:—

"He is so little advanced that he scarcely hears you; but he wishes to have you tell him, if as he says you know anything about it, where he is and how he came here."

'Do you remember any sickness or accident?'

Mary then wrote for him in reply:—

"I don't know. I was at work. Something happened, and the next thing I knew, I was wandering around in the dark and trying to find some way out."

'Well, when that something happened, you lost your material body, you died. And now you are in the spirit world.'

"I don't believe it! Damn it all, why don't you help me?"

'That is what we wish to do. But you must be patient. Can you hear anyone near you?'

"There is a mumbling sound; but they don't know anything. I tell you I want to get out of this!"

'But if you will listen they will tell you how.'

"I tell you they don't! I'm with them, and I can tell!"

'You must be patient if you wish help. You have left the body and are what the world calls dead.'

"No! I know I'm alive! If I can once get out of this I'll show you."

'We wish to try to help you out.'

"I'd *rather* be dead than here!"

'Do you not see some differences compared with what you left?'

"I don't know—I don't seem as large as I was. That's because I can't find anything to eat."

'You say it is all dark. Can you see anything at all?'

"There are queer-looking shadows and a mumbling of voices."

'Did you ever in times past give a thought to what you would do, what you would be like, when death of the body occurred—how you would see, how you would hear?'

"I never gave it a thought. I tell you, I was in the thick of the fight. Lots of opportunities, lots of opportunities for money-making, for the man who knew. And I knew how! I beat them all! And I've got a million somewhere back there that I must take care of."

'What were you going to do with your million?'

"Why, what would I do, except to have a good time? Travel, fun, races, pool—oh, loads of things to do, and a host of ways to spend a million. I made it, I tell you! It was mine to do with as I pleased. And here I am and can't even touch it! Do you call that justice?"

186

'I wonder if you practiced justice in your business?'

"Why, just the same as all businessmen, making money when I could; proud to beat the other fellows to it; proud that I had the judgment to step in at the right time and carry off the shekels!"

'How long have you been in this condition?'

"Not long. Don't know when or how I came—just found myself here."

'Did you have a family?'

"No, I lived alone. But I tell you I had a mighty good suite of rooms! Sporty, maybe you would call them; and sporty they surely were after business hours. You see I was an A-1 businessman, and never let pleasure interfere with business."

'Is your mother living?'

"No, she died long ago."

'Were you ever married?'

"No, never wanted to."

'Do you remember your mother?'

"Not much. She died before I got grown up."

'Do you remember any good things you did during your life, any help to anyone?'

"Gee! I don't know. Yes, I do! I had to help a poor woman once who was burned out, and had nothing to feed herself or her children until some of us fellows got in and made up a purse for her."

'Did that give you any pleasure?'

"I don't know. I don't remember much of that."

'Did you do anything else?'

"I used to give to churches and charity when asked, because it reacted favorably on my business. Oh, well now, I remember one thing I did: helped a blind girl to have an operation on her eyes. My, but she was grateful! Didn't cost me much either. Wish I had done more of that sort of thing."

'If you had, you might have had more happiness.'

"Bet you can't tell me any way toward happiness in this hell of a place!"

'Well, if you want to get out of that place, and wish us to help you, you must do as we say. Now tell us more about what happened when you left your business and came here.'

187

"I was in my office. Someone came in. Said I had—(the impression was to write the word 'cheated')—No, I won't write that word. It wasn't so! I only did what any smart businessman would have done, made a little money on the side. But it happened to clean him out, and he blamed me. He pitched right into me. I don't remember whether it was pistol or fist. But the next thing I knew I was here! That's all the story."

'Well, it is very clear from what you say, that he killed you. That is, your body was killed, but you are still alive. Only now you are in another world under other conditions. Do you not see the difference?'

"I see my hands do not look the same. I can see through them. Well, suppose I am dead! What are you going to do about it?"

'Help you, if you will let us. You say you want to get out of that dark place?'

"You bet I do! Tell me how."

'Now listen carefully. Do you hear anyone?'

"Y-e-s, I do. Who is it?"

Then after a moment:—

"Someone here is telling me that I can come into a beautiful life if I will try. But that I must give up selfish thought, and try first of all to help others. But, how can I do that? I can't even help myself!"

'If you will listen carefully to what they tell you, you will learn how.'

"I begin to hear words plainly. Yes, and I begin to see plainer! Why is that?"

'You are beginning to learn how to use your spirit powers.'

"Is that true? Well, I guess I'll have to believe it. But there is my old life! It looks kind of bad to me now. I never saw it look so before. Yes, I'll try to be a better man if you will help me."

'We cannot be with you. But Mary is trying to help you already.'

"Where is she?"

'Right by you. Do you not see her?'

"Yes, I begin to see her. Why! She is dressed in silvery white! Someone else is with her. Will they help me?"

'Of course they will, if you will let them.'

"Well, I'll try."

THE SHOP GIRL

"We have brought a young woman to you who seems to feel that she has been injured in some way. We are not certain whether it is a physical or a mental hurt. But she still thinks she is living, and she is full of hate and revenge against someone."

(This proved to be more fear than hate.)

'Can she hear you?'

"We think not."

We then spoke to her:—

'We are told that you wish assistance. Can we help you?'

"Who are you?"

'Friends who wish to help you.'

"Where am I?"

'Are you lost?'

"Yes."

'How did that happen?'

"I have been as if in a dream. I was trying to get away from someone, and I must have lost my way."

'Was someone trying to injure you?'

"Yes. A man was hurting me, and I ran."

'Are you injured?'

"Yes. I scarcely know how."

'Where did you live?'

"In— I've forgotten!"

'Was it in a large city?'

"Yes."

'What did you do?'

"I was working in a shop."

'Was that where you were hurt?'

"I hardly know. I think it was somewhere else."

'Can you tell us about it?'

"I forget. I think I was going home. I think someone seized me, and I remember struggling, and I remember my head hurting me. I was running away, and I must have lost my way."

'Probably when the man seized you he hit you on the head and caused your death.'

"Oh, that cannot be!"

'Yes, you are still living, but are in the spirit world.'

"You do not know!"

'Yes, it is true. Are there people near you?'

"Yes, there are many."

'Can you hear them?'

"No, I hear nothing. They are staring at me, and some seem trying to talk, but I hear nothing."

'Do not be frightened. Listen to them carefully. Can you hear them?'

"I hardly know."

'Try again. Be patient.'

"Yes! I hear a sound!"

'Isn't a lady trying to tell you something?'

"Yes! I hear her. She says I am dead! I don't understand!"

'She will help you. She will be your friend.'

"She says she will help me."

Then the leader of the circle wrote:—

"We are comforting her, and are sure she will understand now. She is so frightened we can hardly make her understand. But she will soon comprehend."

THE SPORTSMAN

"We have someone here who needs help. He has not been here long, cannot adapt himself at all to conditions, and does not understand anything of this life."

'Can he hear?'

"Not well, but a little."

'Can he see?'

"Just a little. We have been trying to help him, but he perceives so little of spirit impressions that we have brought him to you. We will write for him."

'Well, friend, what can I do for you?'

"Who are you?"

'We are friends who wish to help you.'

"Where am I?"

'You are in the spirit world. You have left the earth life.'

"No, not that. I know it is not so, for I can walk, move, and now I can talk to you."

'How did you get where you are?'

"I don't know. I suppose I may have lost my way. But I don't understand it. I have a pretty good sense of direction. How did I get here?"

'You died and left your earthly life behind.'

"No, I didn't, for I am alive now!"

'Did you not know you had a spirit within you?'

"What do you mean?"

'We mean that you yourself never die, though you may lose your body through death.'

"I am not dead, I tell you! Don't be foolish!"

'Where did you live?'

"Well, I was in the East. Well— I guess I was in Florida. I know I was planning to go there. But, how queer! I don't remember how I got there! Did I lose my mind and wander off without knowing it?"

'Were you sick?'

"No, not that I know of. I was with a party of young men. We went fishing somewhere. Where under the sun was it! I don't know!

We were having a royal good time, smuggled a little of the forbidden aboard: some I had bought on the—"

'From 'bootleggers'?'

"Yes, I suppose so. We all drank and had a pretty good time. I think maybe the stuff was not good for me, for I remember now that I felt very sleepy, very sleepy. And I suppose I became unconscious in my sleep. Did they put me on shore while I was asleep? We were— we were— I don't know how I came here. But here I am!"

'Well, either you were drowned, or the liquor was too much for you, for you have died and are now in the spirit world.'

"No! That can't be! I can talk with you and hear you, and I can see, though not very plainly."

'Can you see other people near you?'

"There is someone near me, several of them, in fact. I see them, but not very well."

'Can you talk to them?'

"Haven't tried. What is the use? I don't know them."

'You are talking with us, and you do not know us.'

"You began it! I wasn't asking for you."

'Listen and see if you can hear any of these people.'

"I can hear, I tell you, though not very plainly. There is a woman near me has on fine robes. She is trying to tell me things, but I don't seem to 'catch on'."

'Listen carefully. I think you can understand her.'

"Well, I guess I do hear a little better. My! She has on a beautiful dress! Soft and shiny and flowing; I wonder where she got it?"

'What are you wearing?'

"I don't know. I never thought of that. But, they aren't mine! How did I come by them?"

'There seem to be a number of things you do not understand. Do you not think that perhaps we are right?'

"*What do you mean?*"

This was written very forcibly, as though it was beginning to dawn on him.

'That you are a spirit.'

"No! No!! No!!! I know that isn't so! Someone must have taken me when I was asleep and carried me off!"

'Pretty much like a fairy tale, eh?'

"I don't want a fairy story! I want my own life and my own home."

'You will find we are telling you the truth.'

"No! I can move, talk, and believe me, I'm going to get out of this queer feeling if I can!"

'Have you looked at yourself, at your hands?'

"Why! I am thin! My hands! They are almost transparent! Say!! *What has happened to them?*"

'We have told you what has happened. Did you never hear of spirit?'

"No, never heard of such a thing."

'Did you not know that a part of you went on living after death?'

"Never heard of such a thing."

'Did you never go to church?'

"No."

'Or read books?'

"No. Didn't have time. Used to read the sport papers a little, all about the fights and games, baseball and football and—"

'Did you never think what would happen after death?'

"No. I tried to put that out of mind. It isn't good for a man to think of that sort of thing. When you are alive, why, live! Have a good time! Let the future take care of itself. The preachers talk a lot of stuff a man can't believe. I made the most of my life; had a good business, plenty of money, and jolly good friends. Where are the rest of the boys, anyhow?"

'Doesn't it begin to dawn on you that we may be right?'

"*What the dickens do you mean? And what can I do about it?*"

'We have told you to listen to those about you. Are you not willing to try?'

"*I don't want to stay here. Tell me how to get out.*"

'We have told you. Listen to those near you.'

"This woman dressed in white says I am a spirit now, and must learn the spirit ways of learning and thinking. *Does she mean that*

I am alone; that my old comrades are gone; and I have nothing to do? No business? No pleasure? No— Oh, my soul! This can't be true! What shall I do?"

'We have told you. Listen to the lady who is trying to make you understand.'

"I am a man! I don't want to listen to a woman preacher!"

'Well, I am afraid we cannot help you unless you do.'

"What will she tell me?"

'She will probably tell you that you must be kind to others and learn how to live a different life.'

"I can't be kind until I know where I am, can I?"

'We have told you where you are.'

"Well, I'll take the advice of this one in the white robe. She says she can help me to understand."

Then, as if in reply to something Mary had said to him:—

"All right. I'll try."

THE FOOTBALL PLAYER

"There are many here to be comforted. Can you help? We will let you try, for we have one here who does not know he has died."

'A man?'

"No, a boy. A young boy, hurt in a ball game, and coming over here while unconscious. Speak to him."

Sis asked if she could help him.

"Who are you?"

'I am a friend who would like to talk to you. They told me you were playing ball?'

"Yes, and we were winning too. Why don't they tell me the score?"

194

'Were you hurt in the game?'

"I was knocked out, I know; but what of that! I had been in training, and my muscles were like steel. I don't know why they picked me up and brought me here."

'You did not see all the game?'

"No. I know they won though."

'How do you know that?'

"I heard a voice. Someone called to me and said, 'It's all right! We won!'"

'How were you hurt?'

"In the scrimmage. When I had the ball under me the boys all piled on top of me."

'Oh! It was football?'

"Yes, football. Gee, it was great! They didn't get the ball though; I held onto that."

'Did you see any more of the game?'

"No. I guess they were afraid I couldn't stand the rest, so they brought me here. But I don't like it. Where are the rest of the boys?"

'Do you feel your injury now?'

"Not a bit. Never felt so well in my life. Bet I could hold my own with any of them."

'Do you see anyone near you?'

"None of the boys. Where are they?"

Mary says, "He has not the slightest comprehension yet that he has died."

Sis asked if he could be very brave.

"There's nothing to be brave about. We won; and that is mighty fine. I don't have to pretend any bravery."

'Suppose I should tell you that in that scrimmage you were injured so severely that you died?'

"I'd say you lied. Oh! excuse me! But I couldn't help it."

'No, it isn't a lie. It is the truth.'

"No, I know better."

'Have you looked at yourself?'

195

"Where are my togs? I never dressed like this!"

'That is because you have left the earth life.'

"Now you are trying to frighten me. *You can't do that!*"

'What are your clothes like?'

"They are not mine. That's all there is to that."

'You must learn that you are in spirit land.'

"I don't believe it. Tell me the truth."

'Are your parents living?'

"Yes. They were on the grounds too. Where are they?"

'Where did you live?'

"I lived in, or rather near New York."

'Were you playing ball in New York?'

"No, at our own ball grounds. We had a match with another school."

Then Mary wrote:—

"We think we will wait and bring the boy another time. He needs careful guidance. We think he was a bright boy, with great ambition in athletics, as well as in his studies, and we do not wish a shock to come to him too suddenly. He will think of what you have said, and by and by we will go further and convince him that he has left his earth life. You need not expect him to fall gently into the idea that his earth life is over, and he is to begin again in an unknown world, with unknown laws of which he has never dreamed."

At another time we talked to him again.

"We have brought him. He is a bright boy, but still in a mystified condition."

'Can he see or hear?'

"Not well. He knows there is a personal and friendly influence near him that in some way comforts and directs him. But beyond that he has not comprehended this life."

Sis asked if he could hear her.

"Of course. Where am I? How came I here?"

'You heard us telling you about it when you were here before.'

"Did I? Well, I don't understand?"

'Did you ever go to church?'

"No, not that I remember. There was a church, and some of my pals went to Sunday School, but they never said anything about it."

'Why did they go?'

"Because their parents made them."

'You know that people die, do you not?'

"Yes. I've seen the funerals go by."

'Do you know what became of the people after death?'

"Why, they were put in the ground."

'Do you think that was the end of them?'

"Yes. Couldn't be anything else, I suppose."

'Did you never hear that they lived in another world?'

"No. The doctors said they were dead. Dead! That's the end of it, I suppose."

'That was not the end of you.'

"Of course not. I didn't die."

'Yes, the body you had on earth died, and was buried.'

'No! It never was buried!'

"Yes, it was. But you yourself, your soul, went on living."

'No! I didn't die! I know I didn't!'

All through the rest of the talk with him the pencil wrote very emphatically, and Sis's hand was strongly controlled, showing the great excitement under which he was laboring.

'Is your body the same? Look at your hand.'

"Why, no! It's thin! And— why! I can see through it!"

'Could you use it for playing ball?'

"No! What happened?"

'When you were hurt in the football game, you left your earthly body, and it is your spirit, your inner self, that is now talking.'

"How do you know that?"

'Because we have talked with many who are like you. You say you never went to church?'

"No, never."

'Or Sunday School?'

"No."

'Or read the Bible?'

"No."

'Well, if you had read the Bible, you would have learned that death was not the end. The spirit lives on.'

"What is spirit?"

This was explained to him as well as we could.

"My! How do you know?"

'That is what we are taught, and that is what we have learned by talking with others who have been brought to us as you have. You are a spirit, and you will learn that you can enjoy life there, and can improve in every way.'

"Will someone help me?"

'Yes, of course. Did someone bring you here?'

"Yes. Someone, or something guided me here."

'Can you see anyone near you?'

"I see a shadow."

'Keep real quiet and say, 'I am going to see.' Does it help?'

"Well! I do see! How is that?"

'It is your spirit sight, and you can improve it. Will you try?'

"Well, I just guess I will!"

'Now can you see anyone?'

"There are two ladies. Oh, they are beautiful! Will they help me?"

'Yes, indeed. Can you hear them?'

"No. Can they talk?"

'Yes, and if you will listen quietly, you will hear them.'

"I hear a sound... I hear a sound! Can I hear, do you think?"

'Yes, if you will try. Listen for words.'

"They tell me they will take care of me. Do you know them?"

'Yes, we know them well. Will you go with them?'

"Can't you come?"

'No, we cannot come now, but we will probably see you some time. Now go with these ladies, and they will take care of you. Don't you want to?'

"I'd love to."

We talked of him for a time, and then turned to Mary again:—

"He will be all right now, and will be very happy. Dee is entertaining him now."

'Can you tell how his excitement was so strongly conveyed through you to Sis's pencil?'

"We do not know that; but we know that there are unseen powers which respond to our thought. Sis's hand and arm are influenced because of the increased power. Suppose you were suddenly attacked, would not a sudden energy propel something in defense, a something you might not be capable of doing or using normally?"

THE FARMER

"There are so many here who need help. If you can speak to a man who is here, we will try to write what he may reply."

'Have you learned anything about him?'

"We can read some of his thoughts, and believe he was sick and died from tuberculosis. He does not know what has happened, but realizes that he is not in his own home."

'Well, friend, we would like to help you if we can. Can you hear us?'

"Who are you?"

'Just friends. Can you tell us how we can help you?'

"I am not in my own home, and cannot understand why."

'Can you see?'

"I can see that I am in a country that is not familiar to me. It is rather dreary and desolate, but I do not recognize it."

'Where did you live?'

"I live in Illinois. I am a farmer, but have been sick a long time, and have not been able to work. I was very sick the last I remember, but I seem much better now. Only I don't understand why I am in another place."

'Have you a family?'

"Yes, I have a wife and two children. I am wondering why they do not find me?"

'Well, I must tell you that when you were very sick, you died. And you have left your earthly body behind and are now in the spirit world.'

"I don't understand. What do you mean?"

'We mean that you have left your body and are what the world calls dead.'

"I am not dead! I can talk, and can move about."

'Did you ever think what would happen at your death?'

"Why, I would be put in the ground, of course."

'Did you ever hear that your soul would live on?'

"Yes, I think the preachers say something of the kind; but I never took any stock in them."

'It is true, nevertheless. That accounts for your condition now.'

There was a wait of some moments.

Mary says, "You have startled him so he does not know what to say."

'Can you hear me?'

"Yes, I hear you; but what are you telling me such stuff for?"

'Do you see anyone near you?'

"I see some ladies, but I don't know them."

'Can you hear them?'

200

"Why, yes, I do hear some kind of sounds. What sort of a place am I in?"

'You are in spirit land, just as I said.'

"I am sure you are joking."

'Can you hear what the ladies say?'

"Yes, they tell me the same thing."

'Yes, because that is what has happened to you.'

"No! It is not true! I am alive! I can talk and see and move. Dead people don't do that."

Again there was a short pause.

Mary says, "He is so puzzled we cannot make him listen."

Finally he asked:—

"You say spirits can talk?"

'Yes. Do you not hear the ladies near you?'

"They say I am dead!"

'Yes. That is what I am trying to tell you. You were very sick and finally died. Do you not feel well now?'

"Yes, I feel fine. But I don't understand it at all."

'It may have happened some time ago. What year was it that you were so sick?"

"I think it was 1900.'

'1900! Is that right?'

"Yes."

'Do you have any idea what this year is?'

"No."

'It is 1926.'

"Now you are joking!"

'No. It is the truth. Has not the time seemed long?'

"Yes, long enough. But I have not been awake part of the time. I seem to be sort of dazed most of the time. I thought it was because I was sick."

'Had any of your family died before you were sick?'

"I lost my mother."

'Can you hear anyone else near you besides the ladies?'

"I see many."

'Do you see your mother among them?'

"No. I don't see her."

'I am sure you will before long.'

"I think she would not want to see me, for I was not a good son to her."

'Would you not like to see her?'

"Yes, of course. I do not know any of the people about me, but the lady who first spoke says she thinks she can find my mother."

Then Mary added:—

"We can care for him now. He is still only partly convinced, but as we can now make him hear, we can help him."

ANOTHER BUSINESSMAN

"We wish to have your help just now, for we have a friend who has not recovered his sight or hearing since he came. Will you help him? We will write for him. We think he will respond to your words, as he is still so much in the earth vibrations."

'Friend, we hear you need help. Can we assist you? Can you hear me?'

"Yes, I hear a voice, and it is a joy. Who are you?"

'One who may help you.'

"Who are you?"

'One who can tell you that you have left the earth life.'

"No, I have not. How should I leave it?"

'Well, you have not left it by airplane or balloon, but by death.'

"What do you mean. I have a body. Don't you see it?"

"No, I do not see it. I only hear your voice."

"Why is that?"

'Because you are a spirit and I am not.'

"What do you mean?"

'Your body has died, but your soul is alive.'

"No! You are wrong, horribly wrong! For I am here, body, voice, feeling and all. Can't you see me?"

'No, I do not see you. Tell me how you look, and who you are.'

"I am about thirty years old, had a good business, but was taken ill, and I suppose when ill I just wandered away."

'Were you in bed?'

"Yes."

'Dressed?'

"No."

'What have you on now?'

"I am dressed! How did that happen?"

'What are your clothes like?'

"I never saw anything like them. They don't look like a man's clothes at all. Who rigged me up like this?"

'Tell me what you are wearing.'

"It is a sort of loose, flowing robe, maybe like a Roman toga. Who dressed me, and what for?"

'You have left the body and are now in spirit land.'

"Where is spirit land?"

'Where you are.'

"Where are *you*?"

'I am on earth.'

"So am I."

'What are you standing on?'

"Standing on! Why I suppose soil, or grass, or something. I can't see it very well, but I know I am on a firm foundation."

'Do you see anyone near you?'

"No, I wish I could. I am lost, and no one near to tell me where to go."

'Do you not see a lady near you?'

"No, I don't see anyone."

'What were you doing before you were ill?'

"I had a store. Business was good, getting ahead. Then I took sick, fever, and got very weak. I went to sleep, and must have slept a long time and slept very soundly, for the nurse must have dressed me up in this way and let me walk around. And so I lost my way. Why doesn't the nurse come for me?"

'You will never need a nurse again.'

"Why not?"

'Because you will never be sick anymore.'

"Gracious goodness! How do you know?"

'Because spirits do not get sick.'

"What do you mean?"

'Did you ever think of a hereafter?'

"I used to go to church sometimes, but I didn't care for the sermons."

'You have left your body, and are now living in spirit.'

"Why should I see my body then? For I have hands, arms and limbs; can talk and hear you, though I do not see you."

'Keep still and listen.'

"Why should I? I'd rather get on my way to my home and family."

'You cannot go back.'

"Oh, can't I? We'll see about that!"

'I am telling you the truth. You will never go back to your home.'

There was a long pause, and finally Mary wrote:—

"He is almost stupefied at this revelation."

After a little he wrote excitedly:—

"Help me! Help me to understand! What am I to do? What can I do? I'm not in heaven or on earth. Where am I?"

'You are where souls go at the death of the body. Can you listen?'

"I'll try. I hear a little. Someone is telling me I am in soul life now. What and where is soul?"

'The one who is near you we call Mary. She will tell you.'

"She says she will help me to understand. But how?"

'Listen and you will find out.'

"Will she tell me? Will she stay near me?"

204

Mary says, "We can take care of him now. He will soon see and all will be well. He is not bad, only material-minded, and no perception at all of spirit life and spirit thought and action."

THE TRAVELING MAN

"Here is one who has entered into this life without any comprehension of its value. Will you try to help him? He can hear earth sounds, but not spirit voices."

'Friend, do you know where you are?'

"No, I wish I did. I seem to have wandered a long time, and I am very tired."

'What caused you to wander?'

"That is what I would like to know. I have heard of people losing their memory, but I had no thought that I should have that trouble."

'Were you ill?'

"I think so. I remember a hospital and a doctor."

'Did you have friends?'

"No, I haven't what you might call friends. I had no family, no near relatives, and I never comraded with men. I don't know why; guess I liked my own ways or thoughts or ambitions best."

'Did you grow worse when sick?'

"I suppose I did, and that is probably what is the matter: I lost my mind and wandered away."

'Do you know that you have died?'

"What? No, I don't! Nor you, either! I am as much alive as you are."

'Yes, but you are a spirit.'

"Spirit! Well! What do you mean by that?"

'Did you not know that you had more than a physical body—a spirit, a soul?'

There was quite a pause, and then Mary wrote:—

"He is so ignorant, or so utterly thoughtless in regard to the deeper life of mind and spirit, that your words have not taken effect. Go on."

'What do *you* think is wrong?'

"I'm blessed if I know! That is what I want you to tell me."

'Can you hear?'

"I can hear you, but I cannot see you very plainly. But you are in some city, in some room. Tell me where, and how I can get there."

'Did you never think there would be something left after death?'

"There couldn't be! I've seen dead people! There's nothing there to live."

'Have you read what the Bible teaches?'

"Never read the Bible. It's an old book, and no one believes it now; just full of old stories that can't be true, so I've heard men say."

'Where did you live?'

"Somewhere in the West. I don't seem to remember exactly. But I didn't stay in one place long. I was a traveling man, had things to sell."

'What would you say if we told you that you are now in California?'

"I'd say I must have stolen a ride on some train."

'No, you have died and your spirit is in California.'

There was much excitement shown by the pencil, and it finally wrote:—

"No! I'm not dead and buried! Why! How can you talk that way? You are a fool!"

'Look at your hands.'

"What's the matter? I grew thin while I was sick, I suppose."

'How about your clothes?'

"Well! You've got me now! Someone has dressed me up in new clothes. Who did it, and when?"

'Can you see anyone about you?'

"No. I have pretty nearly lost my sight... Yes, by looking hard I can see two people standing near me."

'What do they say?'

"They don't tell me anything."

'Listen again. Do you not hear a voice?'

"Well… yes, I guess so. No words though."

Then, after a moment, the pencil wrote very emphatically:—

"I don't want to hear! I won't believe it! She says I am dead! Great goodness! What a lie! Take her away! I don't want to listen to such talk!"

We carefully explained the conditions to him, asking if the peculiarities and discrepancies did not indicate that we were telling the truth. Finally Mary wrote:—

"He is thinking about it now and we can help him."

'Can you hear now?'

"Yes, I can hear, and they tell me I *am* a spirit, and that I can be a happy one. Oh, Lord! How can I understand this!"

We explained further, and after a little, he wrote:—

"Well, here I am, if this is so. I am as helpless as a newborn babe. But here goes! I'll try."

THE MILLWORKER

"We have found a woman who is wandering alone and crying out for help, that someone is killing her. We have succeeded in quieting her, but not in helping her to realize that she is in spirit life. Can you speak to her?"

'I am a friend. Do you wish help?'

"You may be an enemy. I have no friends."

'What did you do? Why should you not have friends?'

"I didn't do anything. Everyone was cruel to me."

'Did you not love people?'

"No. I never loved anyone."

'Did you ever try to help others?'

"No. Why should I?"

'It might have made you happier.'

"No it wouldn't. I had all I could do to take care of myself."

'What were you doing?'

There was no reply from her, but Mary wrote:—

"We think, from reading her thoughts, that she was a worker in a mill, and thought she was being persecuted by other workers."

'Do you know where you are?'

"No."

'Can you see anyone near you?'

"No. I am in the dark."

'Who brought you here?'

"I came alone. I was just wandering around and you talked to me. But I can't see you, and I don't know who you are. But you needn't try to hurt me. I won't stand for it! *I can fight anybody who tries to 'come it' over me!*"

'Nobody wants to hurt you now. We want to help you if we can.'

"Nobody wants to help. They are all mean and cruel."

'If we could help you to see, would you think we were friends?'

"Maybe. Maybe you would try some trick on me?"

'No, never. We feel sorry for you.'

"No one feels sorry for me! They are all just the same—bad and cruel."

'Isn't that because you think bad thoughts?'

"No!"

'Suppose you try to think a kind thought and see if it will not help.'

"What would I think? I don't know of one."

'Try to think someone is near you who wants to help you.'

"I don't believe it!"

'Try it. Keep thinking it.'

"Why should I?"

'Because good thoughts help you.'

"That's funny! Never heard that before."

'Are you saying it?'

"Yes, I'm saying it. Don't do any good though."

'Keep trying it. Keep saying, 'someone is kind to me.''

"*There's a streak of light out there! What is it?*"

'Your thought is helping you to see. Keep on saying what I told you.'

"Well, I'll try. I'll keep it up, all right. *I can see a broader light! Someone is standing there!*"

'That is your friend.'

"No. I can't believe it."

'Keep saying it.'

"Will it come true?"

'Of course it will.'

"Well, I'll say it a thousand times if it will work that way. I see someone there! She says she will help me and there will be no more cruel ones. Is that right?"

'Yes, it will be all right.'

"Well! Where am I, that such a thing could happen?"

'Were you sick?'

"No. I was turned out of the mill though."

'Do you remember what you did that you were turned out?'

"I guess I forget. I don't know. Only there was a sort of a strike, and everyone got to fighting, and I hit back—and—and— Why! I don't know the rest!"

'When you hit back you were probably hit and killed.'

"Why, I wouldn't be talking if I had been killed!"

'Did you not know that you had something within you that lived after the body was killed?'

"What?"

'A spirit. Did you never hear of that?'

"No."

'You are a spirit now.'

"How do you know?"

'Because of what you say. Can you see any better now?'

209

"Yes, a little."

'Look at your body. What is it like?'

"I haven't got much. *I've grown thin! What's the matter? I haven't on my dress! Everything is different!*"

"You have your spirit body, and have spirit clothes."

"I think I see the one you say will help me. Will she take care of me if I promise never to fight again?"

'Yes, indeed. You will be cared for.'

Then Mary said they would look after her and would soon make her understand.

THE BOY

"We think you might get something from a boy here. He is newly arrived in spirit consciousness, but does not feel that he is in heaven yet. He can see a little and hear a little. Maybe if he talks to you it will seem plainer. I will write for him. I have told him that a friend on earth can speak to him. He says, 'How is that? No one there can speak to anyone here!' He has never heard of any connection between the two worlds. He says, 'Can I talk with someone there?'"

Sis said she would be glad to talk with him.

"Well, tell me where I am. All seems so strange. And I have died, they tell me; yet I know I am alive!"

'Did you not know when here that you had a spirit body as well as a material body?'

"No, I never believed that. I used to go to Sunday School too, sometimes; but that was to learn about God, and about the ways we could serve Him."

'Were you very sick?'

"No, I was drowned: fell from a boat, somewhere in a warm climate. I am an American, all right."

'Was it in Florida?'

"Yes, that is it. It was the upper part of Florida. They tell me I will learn things. I hope so. I went to school over there, but wasn't a very good scholar; didn't like it, rather go fishing."

'Well, I doubt if you will be able to go fishing anymore, but you will find many other fine things to do.'

"There is a lady here who says I will grow, and grow in power of thought, and will then be happy, happier than I was on earth. I had a pretty good time back there. Wish I was back there now."

'You will have a good time where you are when you learn a little more about things.'

"But there isn't any ocean, or any sailing, or fishing, or anything! What can a boy do to amuse himself?"

'Did you ever travel when here?'

"Not much; only auto rides about the country."

'Do you see anyone near you?'

"I see a lady—I see two ladies near me, and they tell me I am going to hear better and see better, and then I can do things. That will be fun. But it's queer, though! I haven't got the same body I had! I haven't got much of a body anyway—so light and sort of thin! But they tell me it will be all right, and that this body can do things my other body couldn't do. They say I will have lots of fun after awhile. Do you think so?"

'Surely I do!'

"I used to play ball, and tennis too. We can't do that here."

'Well, you must study to learn how to see and hear, and to use all your powers. Then I am sure you will find other things that will make you happy.'

"I guess I shall have to do them before I believe in them."

'Can you hear better than you did?'

"Yes, I am hearing the one who calls herself Mary. She tells me lots of things."

'Wouldn't you like to study and learn how to help other boys who come over?'

"I don't know—maybe so."

Mary says, "His spirit life and activity have not yet really begun. He is just a boy! But he will be all right soon."

THE WASHWOMAN

"We have brought a woman who needs help. We wish you to tell her of this life into which she has come without preparation. She does not hear us yet."

Sis spoke to her, saying:—

'I am a friend who would like to help you. Do you know where you are?'

"No, I am lost. Can you show me the way?"

'How did you find me?'

"Someone brought me, or asked me in some way. I am so confused I do not know where I am, or who the people are that I see dimly about me."

'How long have you been lost?'

"Not a great while, but I don't know how I came here."

Sis then suddenly had a mental perception of a middle-aged woman, unattractive, and with no signs of spiritual, or of much mental, power.

'Can you tell how you came to be lost?'

"I do not remember, except that I was sick and friends were trying to do something for me. I suppose I lost my mind and wandered away."

'How does the place you are in appear to you?'

"It is so dark I cannot see much, but nothing beautiful seems to be near—just dreary-looking country."

'Did your friends think you would get well?'

"They seemed to think I would die. But I fooled them, you see!"

'Suppose I should tell you that you really did not fool them, but that you did die?'

"I would not believe it. The dead cannot talk. We know that the talking apparatus goes down into the grave."

'Well, the people who are near you wish to help you.'

"How do you know?"

'Because I can talk with them.'

212

"Who are you, anyway?"

'I am just a friend on earth who wishes to help you.'

"And yet you said I was dead. You talk foolishly!"

'Did you ever hear of spiritualism and spiritualists?'

"I heard of them, but know they were merely ignorant, foolish people."

'Some were; others were wise and studied the spirit life into which you have entered.'

"I am not a spirit. I have a body and can talk!"

'Did you have a home?'

"Yes, but not a happy one. My man drank. We were poor and I took in washing."

'Have you done any washing lately?'

"No. I got lost some way and cannot find either home or work. Why don't you help me to go home?"

'Did you love your home?'

"No, but it was better than this."

'But you had to work there?'

"Yes, but I got pay for it, and could get things to eat."

'Are you hungry now?'

"No, I have not been hungry, though I have not had food for a long time. I do not see any food or fruit or anything to eat. That is queer!"

'You are where people do not eat much. You are in another condition from what you experienced in earth life.'

"Yes, you told me something I do not believe."

'It is true. When you were sick you entered the spirit world.'

"Spirit world! Where is that?"

'It is not quite heaven, but you will advance and enter there in time.'

"Will I have to work?"

'Not as you have worked. Can you hear now?'

"No, not much. They seem to be talking too."

'Listen carefully.'

"I cannot hear words, just a queer sound."

Then after a few moments:—

"Someone calls herself Mary. Who is she?"

'She is the one who will help you. Can you tell me your name?'

"No, I forget... Yes, it was... No, I can't call it. That is queer!... I hear a sound, and someone says her name is Mary. She asks if I can hear. I do hear now, a little. Yes, I hear her now, and she says I will see as well as ever, and hear too."

Then Mary told us:—

"She will come slowly into a perception of this life. She was ignorant and worldly—that is, worldly with what intelligence she had. And when she comes into consciousness of this life, it will be as a young child. We have many such. They are brought into true spirit life very slowly, and teachers have to be very patient with them. But that is part of our work, and we are glad to help."

THE GIRL

"We know you wish to be helpful. Can you help now?"

'I am glad to do all I can.'

"We have brought a young girl. She has known no spirit life, and apparently has never known a spiritual thought or impulse. Help her to hear and see, that we may be able to teach her. We will write for her."

Sis said she was a friend and would like to help her. Immediately the pencil wrote:—

"Where am I?"

'Can you see?'

"Not much. How came I here? Was I kidnapped? Where am I?"

This was apparently written in much excitement.

214

'Where were you before you came to this place?'

"I only know that I was in bed in a hospital. 'Flu,' I guess. Maybe something else."

'Have you parents?'

"Yes, they took me to the hospital. How came I to leave? Did someone steal me from there?"

'You were very ill, and passed out of your body in what the world calls death.'

"No! I don't believe that! I had nothing to die of."

Mary, the leader of the circle, wrote that she probably also had heart trouble.

'Before you went to the hospital did you ever have trouble or fatigue or dizziness when moving rapidly?'

"Why, yes. I couldn't dance as long as I wanted to. Sometimes I got faint when walking."

Mary wrote that she thought the girl came over suddenly from heart trouble.

'Did you ever consult a doctor about it?'

"Yes, but I couldn't follow his old directions; they would have made an old woman of me. And, besides, the boy I went with— what was his name? I can't remember! That's funny— Well, anyway, he was a regular fellow! Danced wonderfully, took prizes in roller-skating, ran races, and all that. What would he have done if I hadn't gone the limit in dancing? Why don't he inquire for me, or come and see me?"

'Because he knows he cannot find you, for you are what the world calls dead.'

"Who tells me that?"

'A friend is telling you.'

"You don't know!"

'Yes, I do know. I know the symptoms. Can you hear?'

"No, only I hear you a little."

215

'Can you see?'

"Not much."

'That is because you are in spirit life.'

"I don't believe it. What is spirit life?"

Sis tried to explain, only to be met with:—

"I don't believe it!"

'Can you see me?'

"Why don't you come nearer so I can see you? I don't like to be in the dark."

'You are a spirit now, and before long you will be able to see with spirit sight.'

"I must have lost my sight when I was in the hospital. But I guess I am going to get it again, for I can see a little better now. I can see people like shadows moving about near me. *Oh, I see two ladies near me! They are prettier and more beautifully dressed than I ever was!*"

Mary wrote:—

"We can help her now to express herself. She has been talking according to her mortal knowledge or taste. We brought her to you because we could not impress her without some kind of mortal assistance."

THE LONELY NEWCOMER

"We have brought one to you who has come to this life wholly undeveloped spiritually, and he is lonely and afraid. Can you help him?"

Then Mary went on:—

"He was a businessman who thought he was all right for that life or any other. He was honest, upright, and industrious. But even these

216

qualities do not always make the entrance here easy for a human life. He wishes to talk with a mortal, and so we bring him to you. Will you help him to say whatever he wishes?"

After a few seconds of waiting, he wrote:—

"I am here. I came in an accident, therefore had no preparation. Perhaps you will say that the earth life is given us for preparation. But what with business—yes, an almost strangling business life— with recreation only for its help to remove the scars of business worry, there didn't seem much time for..."

There was silence for a time, as if gathering strength to continue.

"Yes, I *am* here, and am truly trying to talk across the silence to one who is still in *that blessed human life!* How unlike this life is to our glorified descriptions of heaven—darkness, misunderstanding, hearing blurred to the last extreme. What am I to think? What am I to think?"

There was another short wait.

'Have you a body?'
"Yes, a sort of one; and it moves easier than my mortal body did. But I do miss the old machine! I knew how to manage that, and where to go. But here! I can't find my way, or the home that I supposed, in some spirit fashion, I might find here. This cannot be heaven, surely! Where am I?"
'When you came into your mortal life as a baby, did you understand where you were, or could you understand what your tiny life meant to you?'
"No, of course not."
'Well, cannot you see that you are just a little child in spirit life, and must wait a little before you understand?'
"Perhaps. But how can I begin?"
'Is there no one there to tell you?'

"Yes, they try to tell me, but I cannot hear them as I hear you. And I cannot see very well."

'But someone is there who brought you to me?'

"Yes, and he seems to be the right sort, and I begin to see him a little plainer. I can hear him better too! And he looks—oh, *far finer*, far finer than any human being I ever saw. Is he a spirit?"

'Yes, certainly. He is a spirit friend.'

"Well! He tells me that I am a spirit, and that if I will stop looking backward toward the earth life, and look forward to this one, that I will come into more power and more joy than I ever knew on earth."

After a few moments of silence, his guide wrote:—

"He is thrilled just now because suddenly his spirit vision opened out, seeming like a cloud suddenly passing away from the sun and letting the glorious sunshine illumine all things. He says:—

"Is this the beginning? Praise God, if this be so! I will live. I will live! And find the glory and joy of this life."

THE WANDERER

"So many spirits are here who wish to be recognized that we do not know whom to allow. We will try one who has never written before. He has not acquired his spirit powers, and may not be able to tell you who he is. He is very anxious to communicate, but his powers are very weak."

The pencil scrambled about over the paper as if someone were making great efforts to write.

Then Mary wrote again:—

"This is a pitiful case. He is struggling with morbid thoughts, has not advanced enough spiritually to be able to express himself, but he longs greatly to speak with someone on earth."

'Has he been there long?'

"Not long. We brought him from another circle because he longed so for communication." He says:—

"For the love of humanity, help me to understand! I do not know the first letter of the heavenly alphabet. I am a wanderer, thrust into this life through accident, with no preparation. What shall I do?"

'Can you hear anyone?'

"Yes, one who calls herself Mary."

'What does she tell you?'

"I can't make out. I don't know. I don't understand."

'Why are you so unhappy?'

"I cannot explain. There is nothing here to enjoy."

'Is there no beauty of scenery?'

"No. All is gray."

'Are there no people?'

"Yes, there are some. But they do not speak to me. I am alone, and I ..."

'Is there anyone you know?'

"Not a soul."

'What would you like most?'

"I would like to hear and see, and find my way, and have some friends. *Why am I here?*"

Again the pencil raced over the paper without making any intelligible words.

'Are you aware you are in spirit life?'

"Well, maybe."

'Try to listen to Mary.'

Then Mary wrote:—

"He is beginning to hear a little. Try to send a thought to him that he is going to hear and see and be happy."

'Can you tell us your name?'

"All my life seems to have slipped away. What good is my name?"

'You still have a personality.'

"Yes, but they do not call me by my name here."

'Listen again.'

"I hear a little."

'Keep it up.'

'I surely will. I do see better! It is going to work!'

'Keep on trying.'

'Will I be happy? Are you sure?'

'Of course.'

"Well, I'll be d-----d!"

'You are surprised?'

"Yes. It's coming! I can see Mary now, and can see others. Maybe you are right."

Then Mary again wrote:—

"He will be all right now, and we can care for him until he comes into his true spirit life. He has been dazed and unhappy for a long time, because he had never given a thought to death, to spirit, and to spirit's requirements and advancement. The life here is so wonderful that it is hardly strange that one who has been immersed in worldly occupation and thought, until all else is starved out of their nature, would be unhappy here at first. If we could only get this truth over to the world and induce human beings to begin their heavenly life there, such suffering would be avoided."

THE CHILD

"Mary will write for a child who came over before anyone had really taught her of this life, and she wonders where she is, and why she is separated from her brothers and sisters."

'Is she here now?'

"Yes. You can speak to her."

'Do you know where you are, my dear?'

"No. I do not know. I am lost."

'Where were you?'

"I was in bed, and a doctor came and gave me some medicine, and I went to sleep. And when I waked up I wasn't sick anymore, but I wasn't home anymore either."

'Where did you live?'

"I lived at the South. But this country does not look like it. It is pretty here though."

'What do you see?'

"Oh, flowers and trees and water."

'Are these near you?'

"There are some, I think; but my eyes seem to trouble me, and I can't see as I used to. I want my mama and daddy and Jim and Charlie."

'Who are Jim and Charlie?'

"My two brothers. Don't you know them?"

'No, I don't know them. How old are you?'

"I was nine my last birthday. I wish I could go home to my mama."

'What shall I tell her, Mary?'

Mary wrote, "Mary will bring some children to talk to her as soon as she can hear them, and they will teach her games, and play with her, and she will be happy."

Then Sis spoke again to the child:—

'Can you hear anyone?'

"No. I don't hear anyone. ... Yes, I do hear a little! I guess I am better. I was sick, you know, and maybe I could not hear well. Someone says her name is Mary, and that she will help me until my mama comes. When will she come? When mama comes, will I have a home, and have my dog and canary and my brothers?"

Then Mary wrote:—

"She is beginning to hear now, and Dee will love to take care of her."

'Yes, I am sure you will, Dee.'

"Yes, I will take care of her and love her until she is happy and contented to stay with us. She is a dear little thing, and it will be a joy to take care of her."

'Is this Dee?'

"Yes, this is Dee. She shall not go about mourning because her family are not here. I will have to be all to her, I guess—father, mother, brothers, and dog and canary!"

'Well, you can do it.'

"Yes, believe me, I can!"

THE VICTIM OF BAD LIQUOR

Another helpless spirit was brought for help. After asking him one or two questions without receiving any reply, he asked:—

"Who are you?"

'A friend who may be able to help you.'

"I am lost. Can you tell me where to go?"

'Where were you before?'

"I was sick and in a hospital. I guess I deserved what I got, for I had lived pretty fast, and had not been very careful in obeying the law."

'You mean by drinking liquor?'

"Yes. We thought it fun to fool the… the ones who were investigating our city. We were in a big city. I don't see how I came to be lost. I suppose I fooled the prohibition officers a little too well, and drank the old stuff until I wandered away. I am sorry I carried it so far. I have learned my lesson, not to drink so much that my mind gets muddled."

'Do you think your mind is unsettled?'

"Why, yes. What else? I'm lost; don't even know what country I am in."

'Can you see?'

"Not clearly."

'Are there any people near you?'

"There seem to be a few, but I guess they don't speak my language, for I cannot understand them."

'How are they dressed?'

"Dressed? Why!… Well!… Gee! I haven't my own clothes! Who played this trick?"

'Was it a trick?'

"Couldn't be anything else."

Then, apparently with an air of suspicion:—

"What do you know about it anyway?"

'Do you wish me to tell you?'

"Yes, if you can. Maybe you are one of those prohibition fellows?"

'No. But I can tell you that you died when you drank that liquor, and are now in the spirit world.'

"No, I'm not! *You lie!* That's what you do!"

'No, I am telling the truth.'

"It can't be the truth! I know I am alive!"

'Yes, but in another world.'

"What in thunder do you mean?"

'I mean that you are what the world calls dead.'

"I'm not! Don't you hear me talking? *That shows of itself! I'm alive!* Don't go on with such nonsense!"

'What do you wish me to do?'

"Help me to get away from this dark place!"

"Do you truly wish me to try?"

"I sure do, if you will stop this fool talk and help me out of this."

'Be very quiet.'

"Why?"

'I can help you better so. Listen.'

"I *am* listening. Can't hear any words."

'Keep on listening.'

"There is a woman talking. What is she here for? *Why, for heaven's sake!* She is telling me I am a spirit! A spirit! Ha! Ha! I drank spirit, all right; didn't know I could turn into spirit!"

'Listen. Be quiet and listen.'

"She tells me I have left my body! Gee whiz! What kind of a place am I in? She says I am in spirit land. Where is that?"

'Did you never hear of spirit?'

"Oh, I heard some people talk about it. Went to a funeral once. One of our boys got killed in a fight. We went to see him planted. We gave him a swell send-off—flowers, music, and everything. But that was the end of him! No getting up out of that ten feet of earth!"

'There was something that did not go into the earth.'

"No!"

'Spirit. That does not die.'

"What are you telling me?"

'The truth. And you won't believe me, yet you are now a spirit yourself!'

"I'm not! *I tell you, I'm not!*"

Mary says he is so stunned, and says: "Ask him again to listen."

'Listen to the lady who spoke to you before.'

"Who is she, the one who is talking?"

'Another spirit like yourself.'

"Another spirit! What?'

Then after a little:—

"She says I will hear her better now. I do hear—but what's the use!"

'She is telling you how to help yourself.'

"I don't believe it!"

He seemed so obstinate that he was taken away. Mary said they could look after him now that he could hear.

There had been a visitor near the circle, it seems, whom Mary was trying to impress. She now said:—

"The visitor is convinced that mortals can help in this way. He has never seen this phase of our work, and we were glad to give him this opportunity. He will carry away an experience through which he may help others, and bring other circles into this work."

THE SUICIDE

"We have one who needs help whom we think is a suicide. She has been wandering long in darkness, and cannot see nor hear us. Can you speak to her?"

'I hear you are lost. I am a friend who would like to help you.'

"Well, I am lost, all right. Who are you?"

"I am a friend, as I said. Can you tell us where you are?"

'I am where it is cold and dark and dreary. Why did I come?'

'I suspect you came of your own accord by committing suicide.'

"Yes, I did. I had dreadful trouble over there. But I don't want to remember it now. It was all a foolish love affair. It seems foolish now. I was a young girl, pretty, they said—foolish and vain, I am sure. Why didn't I know better? I thought death ended all, and I looked forward to forgetfulness and rest. But here I am with keen remembrance, and so far from rest that I am wandering to and fro in the dark, and alone."

'How do you know you are alone?'

"I know I am alone because no one speaks to me."

'Can you see?'

225

"I see nothing."

'Have you a body?'

"Why, yes, of course. I can talk, and I have hands and arms, and a face—at least I suppose so; I can't see my face."

'You have your spirit body.'

"What is spirit?"

We tried to explain.

"I never heard that before."

'Did your parents teach you nothing about a future life?'

"No, they never went to church. I never heard what they call a sermon in my life. I went to Sunday School once or twice with some of my girl friends, but I could not understand what it was all about."

'You will have to begin at the beginning and learn to use your spirit powers. Can you move?'

"Yes."

'But you cannot hear?'

"I can hear you."

'Did you know that friends near you have been trying to talk to you?'

"No, I never heard them."

'Can you see anyone?'

"No, I see nobody."

'Please say with all the earnestness you can: 'I am going to hear, I am going to hear.''

"What good will that do?"

'Trust what I say and try it.'

"All right, I will... What is that queer sound coming from a long way off?"

'Someone is trying to make you hear.'

"Is that so? What shall I do?"

'Keep on saying, 'I will hear.''

"I am saying it, all right... I am saying it... Why, the sound is coming nearer! I hear a word or two!... Yes, now I hear someone telling me that I am going to hear! Oh, who would believe it!"

226

THE WOMAN FROM INDIA

"We can give you a few words from one from a faraway country, yet one who knows your language. She was English born, but early went far away to live. We wish her to tell you her need."

Then this newcomer asked:—

"Will you tell me who you are?"

Sis replied that she lived on earth, and in America, but had the gift of hearing words and messages from them.

"I cannot believe that, for why did I not hear when on earth?"

Sis tried to explain that not all mortals had the same gifts; some were musicians, some were artists, etc. Mary wrote:—

"Will you tell her about America; tell her where it is geographically."

In astonishment, Sis asked if she did not know that.

"No. You may indeed wonder. But she does not know because she became a servant, almost a slave, and all knowledge or education was denied."

'How early was she taken to this country?'

"Very young, not far from babyhood. She is asking how you live? Who does your work? Who gets your meals? What do you eat? How do you get about? She saw her mistress carried by servants in a chair of some kind, or sometimes…"

Here the pencil stopped, but Sis received an impression of riding on an elephant. The pencil seemed to accept this interpretation and went on writing:—

"… but not the free, safe traveling of America."

'Can she hear you tell of life in America?'

"We try, but she is too confused to understand."

'Can she read?'

"I do not know."

'Or see?'

"Not well."

Sis then asked her if she could hear.

"Someone is near who tries to tell me things."

'How old were you when you left the earth?'

"Not very old; took fever and died soon."

'Try to listen. Perhaps you can hear words.'

"Someone says I can soon hear. I know I can, for I already hear her."

Then Mary wrote:—

"This is all true. We found her, and learned enough of her history to make us realize that she would be a surprise for you, and we thought it might help to convince you of our reality. We could not talk with her to any extent, but we could read some of her thoughts, and we could guide her to you, and you have recorded the result."

'Did her mistress really ride on an elephant?'

"Yes. We think not often, but the picture was strong in her memory. She was born in England, and taken to India when very young. Her mother was very likely a servant like herself. We are now able to take care of her and make her understand, and will be able to help her in her progress. She has been on this side some time, we think."

THE PRISONER

"We will bring a man for you to help. We have studied his thoughts closely, and believe he was a thief on earth—one who thought the world owed him a living, and who was determined to get it the easiest way. Of course he is not prepared for a spirit life, but he seems to have a mind that should be fitted for better things. We are anxious to see what your questions will arouse in his mind. He thinks he is still on earth, shut up in the dungeon cell of some prison."

We then spoke to him:—

'We understand you are in prison. We are friends and can possibly help you. Can you hear me?'
"Yes, I hear you. What do you want?"
'Do you want to get out of prison?'
"I shouldn't be here. I am wrongly imprisoned."
'How long have you been there?'
"I don't know. I don't think I have been awake part of the time. I don't remember being brought here."
'Where did you live?'
"I lived in Chicago."
'Where was your home?'
"I hadn't any. I just lived as I could."
'Have you ever been in jail before?'
"Yes. Lots of times."
"You must have taken things many times then?"
'Of course I did. I needed to live, didn't I?'
"What was your trade?"
'I didn't work. I was too smart for that.'
"What were you doing just before you were brought here?"
'I was sick. Had T.B.'
'You are not sick now, are you?'
"No, I feel fine."
'Isn't your cell different from those you usually find?'
"Yes. I don't find any walls."

'How do you know you are in a cell? Why have you not walked about?'

"I hadn't tried. It is too dark."

'Do you seem just the same as when you were in jail before?'

"It seems rather queer here. I wonder if I am just somewhere in the dark?"

'You say you were sick?'

"Yes."

'And now you find conditions different?'

"Yes."

'Well, I can tell you that when you were sick, you died.'

"The h--l you say!"

'Now listen. I will explain.'

"I hear you, but what are you talking about?"

We explained that he was a spirit.

"I don't know what you mean."

'I am trying to tell you that you are dead.'

"No! I am not dead!"

'Isn't your body different?'

"How can I tell here in the dark?"

'Are your parents living?'

"Yes, but I don't know where they are."

'Are you married?'

"No."

'How old are you?'

"About thirty."

'Have you seen your mother lately?'

"No, not for years. She writes once in a while, but I haven't been home in years."

'Now listen.'

"What do you want?"

'Listen intently. Listen quietly with your mind.'

"Yes, I hear a sound of some kind… Yes, I hear a woman saying I am not in jail. She says I will see before long."

Then Mary wrote:—

"He is so completely dazed with the thought that maybe he is dead, that he cannot make sense of anything now. He seemed to hear me, so perhaps we can care for him. He will be slow to progress because he was so sure of his own ideas of things. But we think he will want to push ahead now."

THE DISSATISFIED MAN

"We will write for one who needs your help. Can you speak to him?"

'Well, friend, can I help you?'

"I am a soul, I suppose; anyway they tell me I have left my body. But why have I so little power, so little ability to see or hear, or even think? I don't know. I thought the heavenly life supplied all these things. Why is everything here so poor and miserable?"

'You say everything?'

"Yes, so far as I can see; nothing fair, nothing agreeable for mind or body."

'Is your body ill or in pain?'

"No, thank goodness, I left that back there somewhere."

'What caused you to leave your earthly body?'

"It was cancer, I suppose; but hidden where I could not see it, and everyone was afraid to tell me the truth. Oh, Lord! That any created being could suffer so!"

'What was your belief in regard to life?'

"Oh, not much of anything—except that life had been thrust upon me without any desire of my own; and I might as well make the best of it and get what good I could out of the accident of being a long-suffering human."

'Did your human companions think as you did?'

"No one seemed quite as morbid over it as I did, but I tried to have them see it as I did; that we did not owe *anyone anything* for the life which had been thrust upon us; and that we should live and be merry, if possible—which was seldom possible for me."

'How about your parents?'

"They were not to blame, I suppose; just two young things who married in the heyday of life, and were bound to have a good time. They never wanted me anyway, because I interfered with their good times. And I was passed on from one nurse to another, and later from one boarding school to another; and so they got rid of me, for the most part."

'What became of them?'

"They are over there still, I suppose; only they must be rather old by now, and not able to frolic as before. I don't care! Let them find out what life means, if they can! That is the question I am asking now of you."

'Just suppose you could hear and see, with a body free from pain, and a world full of new occupations and enjoyments; would you take that as an answer to your question?'

"You bet I would! But you would have to prove it to me first!"

'It must come by your learning the use of your spirit powers. Can you see at all?'

"Only very dimly."

'Well, use your spirit power in saying, 'My sight is coming to me."

"What good will that do?"

'Do as I say and you will prove its good.'

"All right. It can't hurt me anyway."

The pencil was quiet for a few moments.

'Are you saying it?'

"Yes—and by jiminy, I can see a little better!"

Again a short wait.

"It does work. Great! Great!"

This was all read aloud, and the pencil added:—

"It is all true. And we can add that he is not an old man, just in the thirties. His life had been warped and dwarfed by circumstances of which he spoke, and he was rather more kindly in his mention of his parents than they deserved. He is hearing better now, and we can care for him. We wish to keep him with us for a time, and he will grow into an appreciation of the kindness of this life in general, and of this circle in particular. We may bring him again sometime."

THE CRIMINAL

"We are here."

'Is this Dee?'

"Yes, and Mary and many others."

'You come flocking in a hurry.'

"Yes, we enjoy the talks as much as you do."

'Have you anything new, strange, or wonderful to tell us tonight?'

"We have a strange story to tell you of a man who needs help. He is able to hear us a little, but he insists we cannot help him. We think he was a criminal of some kind. We can read some of his thoughts, and we believe he was a member of a gang of roughs who attacked a man, and while robbing him, the man was killed. But it is a little doubtful if this man was the direct cause. He was arrested and imprisoned for a time, and the confinement caused his death, probably through tuberculosis. He thinks his companions have all deserted him because he was not strong enough to be with them. Now that he feels strong again, he is very resentful at their neglect. We believe he thinks he is back in prison again."

'Is there anything we can do? We would like to help.' The man replied:—

"Yes. I am in jail, and I do not belong here. I served my sentence, and I should be let out."

'You say you served your sentence?'

"Yes. I was let out before my time because I was sick. Now that I am well again, I am put back in jail."

'Who put you there?'

"I don't know. I was sick, and must have been brought here when asleep."

'Were you very sick?'

"Yes, but I am all right now."

'Did you have tuberculosis?'

"That is what the doctor said; but they must have been mistaken."

'No, he was right. When you were very sick you left your earth body and are now in the spirit world.'

"I don't understand. I'm not dead."

'Does not that explain your condition?'

"Yes, but I wonder if it is true. I don't know what to think."

'It is true. You are now in spirit life.'

"But this is not a life that I understand!"

'Can you hear anyone?'

"Yes. Some people have been telling me the same things you have, but I could not see them and did not believe them."

'Did you have a family?'

"No. I was too young."

'Oh. You are a young man?'

"Yes, about twenty."

'Where did you live?'

"I lived in New York."

'What is your name?'

"I... I... My name is Joe."

'What is your last name?'

"I... I don't remember."

'How long was your sentence?'

"Seven years."

'Were you sent up when only thirteen?'

"No, I was about sixteen. I did not stay in jail only about four years. I was sick and they let me out. But it seems I did not live long, for I was only home about two weeks."

'Was that in 1920?'

234

"No, it was before that."

'Did you know it is 1925 now?'

"No! It has seemed a long time, but I did not know it was that long. I think it was some during the war that I was let out of jail."

There was a long wait, and finally Mary wrote:—

"We are trying to tell him what to do. But the realization that he has died seems to leave him in a sort of dazed condition. We think we can care for him, for he will listen to us now. He is overcome with remorse part of the time, and of course that will lead to repentance, after which the change to a better life will come naturally. He will need help and teaching and sympathy, in a way, but we look forward to a long period of remorse before his final acceptance of the spirit life.

"We have watched many such, and they often become our most enthusiastic workers. Undoubtedly, he belonged to the poorer and more ignorant classes, and looked upon money as the chief attainment of happiness."

A SPIRIT WHO IS OBSESSED

"We have brought one who is influenced by other spirits. You have had no experience with such a case. Try to help us now."

'How can I help?'

"First try to get in touch with the spirit. Ask her name."

'Can you tell me your name?'

"No, I have lost it."

'Have you been on that side long?'

"Not very long."

'Have you forgotten your name?'

"I don't want a name! Someone is bothering me. Go away! Go away!"

235

This looks as though the obsessing spirits identified themselves with the victim, for they use the pronoun "me." Mary writes that it was the two spirits speaking. And she added!

"The spirits obsessing her wish you to leave."
'No, I am not going away. You are the ones who should leave.'
"No, we belong here."

Sis asked Mary what to do.

"We think if you talk with them awhile they will be interested and perhaps can be made to leave the patient."
'What are your names?'
"We call ourselves Jack and Jill."
'Well! Have you gotten your pail of water?'
"No, not yet, nor have we tumbled down hill either."
'You had better go up the hill and learn what is about you.'
"We are contented where we are."
'Why not learn how to travel?'
"We can. We have a spirit who carries us about."
Sis again asked the spirit victim if she had lost her name.
"No, I have it."
'What is it?'
"I don't know."
'You have a name, yet cannot tell it?'
"We won't let her."
'You are two bad spirits. You must get out.'
"We won't get out."
'Yes, you will!'
"When will we go? Where will we go?"

Mary wrote: "Tell them to go to another place, another circle, or any other place."

'Are there no beautiful surroundings to which you could go?'
"Yes, but we cannot get there alone."

236

'It would be pleasanter to go alone.'

"Yes, maybe."

'Why do you not go to the beautiful grove?'

"Is there one?"

'And to that beautiful lake?'

"We haven't seen it."

'You should develop your powers so you can travel alone.'

"Will you go too?"

'No, you must go alone. Get out and travel.'

"We might try."

Then Mary added: "We think they will yield soon."

There was no movement of the pencil, and Sis asked what they were thinking about.

"How to go."

'You can do it. Get out!'

"All right. We are going."

"Mary says, they are really going. Tell them more of the things they can see if they go."

'Have you gone to the lake?'

"Not yet."

'Why not go and bathe in the lake?'

"We would like that."

'Move along then. Don't stay here!'

"We can! We are moving! We will go!"

'Keep trying. Do not give up.'

"We are moving. We are going. We are out!"

Then we asked Mary to tell us all about it.

"She is a woman, and has been so obsessed that without them she is very weak; but she will soon be herself. The spirits were not so much wicked as selfish. They did not develop their own spirit powers quickly—just sufficient for them to fasten themselves upon this poor, weak spirit—and she has been their slave for a long time. She will advance now. We will begin her education at once.

"We are glad we had the opportunity to bring such a case to you. They are not very common. We found this poor woman under the control of these spirits, and so thoroughly under their power as to leave little personality of her own. The two obsessing spirits were selfish and lazy, and found that it was easier to use the woman's spirit energy than it was to develop their own, and so they continued."

'Where are they now?'

"We do not know. We may never see them again. They were not of a kind that we were accustomed to work with, so we will let some other circle help them. We have so many different kinds to deal with, we usually work only with those for which we are best fitted."

WRONGLY EXECUTED

"We wish to bring a poor soul to you for help. When we found him he was muttering to himself something about a murder. We think from reading his mind that he was executed for a murder which he did not commit. But he is so dazed we are not sure we are right."

We spoke to him, but there was no reply to several questions.

   'Can you see or hear?'
   "I do not see, and have heard no one. Who are you?"
   'A friend who would like to help you.'
   "I am in trouble—very serious trouble—but you cannot help me."
   'It may be possible if you will tell me what it is.'
   "I am accused of murder which I did not commit."
   'That is too bad. Are you in jail?'
   "No. I do not know where I am."
   'Were you arrested?'

"I was in jail. I wonder how I got out?"

'Were you convicted of the crime?'

"Yes, and I thought I was to be hung!"

'I think the sentence was carried out, and that is the reason you are in your present condition. Do you not think so?'

This seemed to bring all his memory of the event back to him, and he replied so excitedly that the pencil could scarcely write.

"Yes! Yes! I was! What is it? What is it?"

Mary wrote:—

"He is so excited he cannot understand. Wait a moment."

After a little time, he wrote:—

"What shall I do?"

We asked him to listen intently; perhaps he could hear someone who was near.

"Yes. I hear something."

'There are friends near who are trying to tell you what to do.'

"Yes. I hear them. They tell me I will see soon too. I am not in heaven, am I?"

'Probably not yet, but you are on the way.'

"I thought heaven was for good people and hell for sinners?"

'Something like that, only there is no hell such as you have pictured.'

"I will be glad to see and hear."

"Mary says he is in a pitiful condition, hardly able to think. We believe we can make him understand now, but it is too bad that he has received such a shock. We think he was a young man who was naturally upright, but who fell into bad company, and his companions managed to make him suffer for their crime."

THE PEASANT WOMAN

"We will let you try to help a woman who thinks she has died, but she was very religious and thinks she is not in heaven because none of the saints are here to meet her. We think she was a Catholic, and was taught to believe that the saints were looking after her during life. We think she was French."

I spoke to her and asked if I could help her in any way.

"You are strangers to me. Shall I tell you who I am?"

'Yes, we would be glad to know.'

"I was a peasant in France. I was an old woman, and have thought the saints were my friends, and would care for me when I died. I was sick a long time and my daughter cared for me, and I died in her home. I was in a sleep of some kind for a long time. I am awake now, and I supposed I would see the saints and many angels. But I see no one. What is the matter?"

'Can you see?'

"I see a little, but I see no angels."

'Can you see anyone at all?'

"I do not know. Sometimes I seem to see someone, but it is like a shadow and fades away."

'Can you hear anything?'

"No, it is all still."

'Listen very carefully.'

"No. I hear nothing. I do not think there is any sound."

'Look around you carefully. I think you can see better.'

"Yes... I see something. It seems to me they are people. I see two ladies, but they are not angels."

'Because they have no wings?'

"Yes."

'Well, not all angels have wings. These ladies are spirits, and are there to help you if you can hear them.'

"I can see them plainer now. Will they help me?"

'Yes, indeed they will. Can you hear anything now?'

"Yes, I hear you."

'Try to hear the ladies near you. Can you hear them?'

"No, I hear nothing; but they are trying to talk to me. I can see them well now."

"Mary says we cannot make her hear, but she seems to see us, and we will try to make her understand by motions."

'Can you do that?'

"Yes, a little."

Sis said she thought they used music in such cases.

"Yes, but we have not tried it this time. If we cannot make her hear us we will try that later."

I asked what part of France had been her home. She tried two or three times to tell, but seemed unable to remember.

"No, I cannot remember. I was a poor woman and had to work all my life."

'Do you know where we are now?'

"No, I do not know."

'Do you know of America, and of the United States?'

"Yes, I know of America."

'We are in America, and in California, on the western side of America.'

"I am sure you are telling me wrong."

'Because you are French, and you wonder how we could understand?'

"Yes."

I explained that her thought was translated by Mary, and we received it in English, and that our replies were influenced in the same way, so that she could understand.

"Well, I do not know much. It is very strange."

'Can you hear anything now?'

"No, I do not hear."

'Well, these ladies are trying to talk to you. You must try to hear them.'

"Mary says we will look after her. It may be that we will bring her again. It is easier to make such spirits hear by material means if possible. But we will wait now."

A TERRIBLE ACCIDENT

"Before you stop writing we want to have you try to help a young man whom we will bring to you. He is apparently suffering from the memory of some terrible injury."

When he was brought, we explained that we were friends who had heard of his suffering, and would like to help him.

'Can you tell us about it?'
"I had a serious accident, and I am in terrible pain. I was in a mill and was caught by a belt in the machinery and had my arms torn from my body. I have suffered, and am in great agony. *Why do they not stop it?*"

The writing itself showed something of the man's suffering.

'We will have to tell you that the injury has caused your death. But you yourself do not realize that yet. If you can do so, you will soon be free from pain.'
"I don't know what you mean."
'You can hear us?'
"Yes."

We explained again, somewhat differently.

"I ... I ... If I am dead, how can I talk?"

This we tried to explain to him, and then asked if he could see.

"No, I see nothing."

In our explanation we had said that the pain would soon leave him. We asked if this were not true.

"Yes, that is true... Yes, I feel much better."

We asked some further questions, but received no answer. Mary says he is so overcome with it all that he cannot control himself. We again asked if the pain had ceased.

"Yes, it is nearly gone."
'Can you hear anyone near you?'
"No, I hear nothing."
'Listen carefully.'
"No, I do not hear."
'Is there any light about you at all?'
"No... No, it is all dark."
'That is fine.'
"Yes. What shall I do now?"
'Try listening again, very carefully.'
"Yes... I do. Yes, I hear... I hear someone talking. I believe I am beginning to see too!"
'Good!'
"Yes, someone is talking, I am sure... It is wonderful! They tell me I am to hear and see plainly!"
'Do you see anyone near you?'
"No, I see no one. But I hear a lady, and she says for me to be patient, and to always remember that my old body is gone, and all the pain with it."

Then almost immediately, in great excitement:—

"I don't want to die! I want to live!"
'You would not want to live without arms, would you?'
"No … That would not be good."

Mary added:—

"We can take care of him now. We wanted to have him helped, if possible, in order to stop his agony. We could make no impression on him whatever. We think he will not suffer much more, but it may be some time before he can forget it all. We think he did not live long after the accident, and brought all the pain with him. You have helped him very much."

THE AUTOMOBILE ACCIDENT

"We have brought a woman for help who does not know where she is, nor that she has left her physical body."
'Can she hear me?'
"We think so. The earth vibrations are still strong with her. Speak to her."

'Friend, can I help you?'
"Who are you?"
'A friend who would like to help you.'
"Tell me where I am."
'Where were you before you were lost?'
"I was in an automobile accident. I was thrown out, picked up, and carried to a hospital. Why was I sent away alone instead of to my friends?"
'Where were you?'
"Somewhere out in the country. Pretty fast driving—having a good time. Now I am lost."
'Were you hurt badly?'
"I should say so! Broken bones, head hurt, and unconscious for a time. But they did well by me at the hospital. I haven't so much as a

pain. But I seem to be lost! I can't find my home. The surgeons did good work to let me out so soon, but where am I?"

'Shall I tell you?'

"Yes, if you can."

'I must tell you then that you died at the hospital, and are now in the spirit world.'

"No! That isn't so! Can't you hear me talking? Dead! I should say not! Just show me the way home, and I'll show you that I'm a good deal alive!"

'Are you wearing your own dress?'

"Why! Why! They must have put clothes on me at the hospital! But they are not mine. Why did they not give me my own?"

'What are they like?'

"They are sort of gray-looking, and more shiny than mine; but they don't seem to be silk. I wonder what they are made of?"

'I suppose they are the kind that spirits wear.'

"For goodness' sake! What are you talking about?"

'I am trying to tell you that you died at the hospital, and that you are a spirit now.'

"*I did not die!* And I am not a spirit, whatever that is. I am myself; and I want to go home."

'Look at your hand.'

"Well! It is thin and transparent. But that is because I was in the hospital. Why don't you tell me where to go?"

'I can only tell you that you have left your earthly home, and are a spirit, and must learn the conditions of spirit life.'

"*You don't know!*"

'Yes, I do know. You have been brought to me that I might help you to understand that you are a spirit.'

"*Great heavens! I a spirit!* I, alone and without friends. What can I do? What can I do?"

'There are friends near you who will help you. Can you see them?'

"I can see two people near me, but I cannot see them plainly."

'Can you hear them?'

"They seem to be talking to me. They seem kind and gentle."

'What are they saying?'

"Let me listen. Why! They tell me the same that you have! And that I will learn the new life and be happy after a while."

'Will you go with them?'

"I suppose so. I don't know what else to do."

ANOTHER AUTOMOBILE VICTIM

"We can hardly tell who is here now. Someone wishes to write, but he is unknown to us."

'Someone who needs our help?'

"Yes. Mary will write for him. He says, 'Can you help me to understand? I have come out of something—whether a fainting spell, or sleep, or what? Here I am alone. I can see strange shapes about me; I think I hear a little, but all confused. Where are you, and where, oh, where am I?"

We explained that he was what the world called dead, and that he was now in spirit world.

"Mary says he cannot believe this."

We asked if he had been sick.

"No, not that I know."

'Did you have an accident?'

"Just a little one; car turned over on a curve—picked up, I suppose, and taken somewhere, hospital, I guess; didn't suffer any; and here I am, as well as ever, but no hospital, no nurse, no doctor, no home, no friends. Say! What the dickens does it mean?"

We explained again that he was in spirit land.

"Where is spirit land? I am here. I am well. I can't have died! Never felt better in my life."

'Where do you think you are?'

"Why, in some strange country. You see, I never traveled much, and would not know Italy from Ireland, so far as sight is concerned. But if Italy is full of flowers and trees and pleasant sights, as well as exhilarating atmosphere that makes one feel like flying, I guess I must be there."

Mary added:—

"I think he will soon be conscious enough for us to care for him. He has the appearance of having been a decently good man at least, but probably a material-minded one."

'He must have been killed by the accident, for he doesn't seem to have much recollection of anything afterward?'

"Not much: he died almost immediately, we are told."

We asked if he had ever thought of death and of what would happen then.

"No. I didn't pay any attention to that. I was much alive—young, vigorous, happy—and that is what I am now. But I don't know where I am, or how I came here."

'Do you wish us to tell you?'

"Yes, please."

'Well, we can only say as we did before, that you have left your earthly body, and are now in the spirit world.'

"What do you say? You can't believe I am dead! Merciful goodness! This can't be true! I'm alive! Not dead!"

'When you had the accident, you were killed. Your body died, but there was something—the real you—that went on living.'

"What was it? The real I is here, just as I was before."

'How about the clothes you are wearing?'

"*Who put these things on me?*"

'What are they like?'

"I guess some kind of a robe. Must have belonged to a judge or something! I never owned such an outfit!"

'Can you see about you?'

"A little. Someone here says her name is Mary. Who is she?"

'Mary is a spirit who is there to help you to understand the new life.'

"Mary says he is so stupefied by this new thought, we had better wait a little."

'Has he been on that side long?'

"We think he has been unconscious for several months, and is hardly fully awakened now."

"Can you make him understand now?"

"Yes, we think so."

"Shall we ask him any further questions?"

"You might ask him where he lived."

We did so, but he seemed unable to answer, finally saying:—

"What's the matter with my brain? I can't remember! Who will take care of me?"

'The one who said her name was Mary.'

"The one in the white, pearly robe?"

'Yes. Isn't there someone else there also?'

"Yes. One in a beautiful dress. My! I never saw such beautiful dresses before. Will they help me?"

'Of course they will.'

"Mary says we can care for him now."

THE CAMP-MEETING CONVERT

"We would like to bring a woman to you for help. She was a poor woman on earth, and what religion she had was of the most primitive kind: southern camp-meetings, 'getting the glory,' hysteria, and all the rest, until she believed she was one of the elect, and would

248

be received here by Christ himself. Can you imagine her reaction when she came into consciousness and found only her guides, who impressed her, first of all, with their humility? And when she expected a crown of glory, she saw instead kind and loving friends, whom at first she could not appreciate. She has partly recovered from that shock, but is in a state of disappointment, and feels that she has been utterly deceived. Will you ask her some question?"

'Well, friend, I understand you are disappointed with what you have found?'

"I am. What place is this?"

'It is spirit land, where spirits first go when leaving the earth life.'

"Where is heaven?"

'Perhaps if you first find your spirit self, you will the easier find heaven.'

"My spirit self? I gave that to God long ago."

'Are you sure? Did not God give it to you?'

"Not that."

'Yes, it is true.'

"We have been taught better. I got religion. I was converted, and I gave myself to God."

'Do you know what God wishes you to do?'

"Why am I not told?"

'Perhaps that is why I am here?'

"Who are you?"

'I am here to tell you some of the things you should know.'

"Where are you?"

'I am on earth. You are in spirit land.'

"Well! I might know you could not help me! I left the earth, and am waiting for heaven."

'Who told you that you would go directly to heaven?'

"Why, the preacher who saved me."

'How did *he* save you?'

"Why, I went forward to the sinner's bench, and they prayed for us all, and the first I knew, I was shouting, 'Glory! Glory!' That's the way God saved me."

'Are you sure God made you do all that?'

"Of course I am."

'Have you read the fifth chapter of Matthew?'

"No."

'That gives Christ's own words.'

"What are they?"

'One thing He said is, 'Blessed are the poor in spirit, for theirs is the kingdom of heaven."

"I am converted, I tell you! And I ought to be in heaven now!"

'Why? Just because you were down on your knees?'

"Yes, that is the way. That is what the preacher said."

'Shall I tell you what you should do?'

"You do not know."

'Yes, I *do* know.'

"Tell me then."

'You should think kindly of others, and help all who are in need.'

There was no reply, and Mary wrote:—

"She cannot get that at once. Be patient, and keep on talking to her."

'Do you see anyone near you?'

"Yes, there are some shadows."

'These are spirits like yourself.'

"Who are they?"

'They are friends of ours in spirit land.'

"Who converted them?"

'They advanced toward heaven by the heavenly law of kindness.'

"Is that the way?"

'Indeed it is. Can you hear anyone?'

"I hear just a little. What are they saying?"

'What shall I tell her, Mary?'

"Tell her that in spirit land, which is the portal to the heavenly spheres, love is the first requirement."

'Could you hear her?'

"A little. Was she talking to me?"

'She was talking to me and telling what was necessary.'

"What is it?"

'She says you must have love in your heart.'

"How will I get it? Can she talk to me?"

'Yes. Listen to her. Can you understand?'

"I hear her a little… She talks about love. How can I get it?"

'Listen to her. She will tell you.'

"I will try. … She says she will help me. But, oh! Where is heaven, and my crown, and all the rest?"

'You will find the rest later.'

"Well, I'll try. Will it take long?"

'That will depend upon yourself.'

"Well, I will do as she says, anyway."

'Can you care for her now, Mary?'

"Yes, we will care for her. She begins to hear, and her sight is coming. She will be all right. Dee has got her in hand now."

'Will it take a long time?'

"We can never tell. Sometimes there is an inner spirit which receives with astonishing quickness. But this one at present shows little sign of any spirit illumination. She represents many who have been converted in this way. There are grades of intelligence, of course, but she is not the first one representing this type."

A few days later we asked about her. Mary replied:—

"She was very ignorant, and yet convinced that she had experienced true religion. Perhaps you would like to know the rest of the experience. We tried to help her, but she still persisted that she had 'got religion' in the 'great revival,' as she called it. We had to let her go for a time, but finally she came back in a more possible frame of mind, and we tried to give her one idea at a time: that she must listen—listen—until she could hear us say that 'love is the fulfillment of the law,' and that she must set herself to proving this for herself by trying what loving service for others would do for her. She did not see what she could do, so we asked her to tell others who had arrived in perfect ignorance of this life. She finally began her mission, and, to our joy, she began to realize. That was the beginning, and afterwards she became humble. And in that state of mind we could teach her other truths of spirit life. She is growing toward the light now, and soon will come into perfect happiness."

'Some come very quickly, it seems?'

"Yes. As soon as they accept guidance, and can begin to see and hear, the advancement is rapid."

APPENDIX

~

MENTAL PROCESSES

It is after much hesitation that this chapter is included in the book. It will not be interesting to most readers, and has only a little connection with spirit life in general. The attempt to describe mental processes in material terms will seem clumsy and unnecessary to some, and may not bring enlightenment to anyone. But it did interest me, and the manner of its delivery and record is worth relating.

It was written through my pencil in some eight or nine instalments covering several weeks. Scattered in between were many other messages on entirely different subjects, several of them being of importance. I never knew when I took up the pencil what was coming, and if it chanced to be this subject, it always began just where it was dropped before.

I know that skeptics, and especially skeptical psychologists, will attribute it all to my subconscious mind. But to my thinking it stretches this theory beyond the breaking point, and I cannot imagine what other source could possibly be suggested except a spiritistic one. There is not the slightest evidence that it originated in my mind except the fact that some unusual mental feats have been fairly well proven to be the work of a subconscious mind in other instances. So to avoid the spiritistic theory, critics will class this with them, although there is no other excuse for it.

The following is the complete message collected from our records:—

"When a spirit here has need to impress a thought on another, he may use one of several methods. We use speech as you do, but not always. We use signs and symbols corresponding to writing, as you do, but not so often. Many times we simply transfer our thought directly to the one we wish to impress. It is this method we wish to describe, or at least to discuss.

"To get an understanding of such a process, it is first necessary to try to understand what thought is. Here we encounter at the very beginning the greatest problem of all. We cannot in any way explain the process, for it is too little understood even by us. But we can describe some of the operations of thought, though we may not know the complete origin of these operations.

"We have the power, most of us, of seeing these operations. You might compare it with a view of the operations of an intricate mechanism on earth. What we see, however, is not wheels and levers, but just the thoughts themselves. How do they appear? What do they look like, you say? Well, it is more like the forming of a sentence of writing. Not that any words or letters appear, but impressions of words come to us in a way that we can only compare to that of vision. Just what causes these impressions is what we wish to try to explain.

"We have learned that all efforts to think cause vibrations in the ether. These vibrations are just as complex as the waves generated in the atmosphere by the voice, and usually much more so. You have noted, no doubt, when listening to a phonograph, how the peculiar timbre of the human voice is reproduced so perfectly that no difficulty is experienced in recognizing the author of the record.

If you can carry your imagination forward so as to comprehend an ethereal vibration still more complex, you can possibly begin to understand the process of the transmission of thought. So much for the origin.

"Now you will find a greater difficulty in trying to understand how these ethereal waves are received and recorded so as to complete the impression on the mind of the one for whom the thought was intended. Your difficulty will come from the human inability to entirely put aside the conception of the material brain. You must imagine, for the moment, an ethereal counterpart. We are not saying that we have such a counterpart, but you will more readily understand the process by keeping such a picture in your mind.

"Now when a thought strikes this spirit brain it causes a motion to take place—a motion of the particles composing the brain. The motion which is set up varies as the thought which causes it varies. When these moving particles come to rest they adjust themselves in impressions or patterns. Each thought results in a different pattern. When such an impression is formed it remains or persists indefinitely. A new thought does not disturb it. But each pattern, to a certain extent, covers or hides those formed before, and so those formed earliest are most obscured, other things being equal. A strong thought causes a prominent pattern. Such a one is not so easily obscured as more indefinite ones.

"The particles that form each pattern are only an infinitesimal portion of those available. A thought does not cause all the particles to move. You will wonder how an unlimited record is made, for you will rightly imagine that there must be a limit to the particles composing the brain. We can explain this by saying that this is the only thing in spirit life corresponding to the phenomenon of weariness in material life. As these particles are used by incoming thoughts, the depletion causes a condition that might be called fatigue. But with a short rest these are restored from the universal source of all power. We do not know this source sufficiently to enter into any description of it now.

But the new particles arrive from somewhere and build up or replace the portion used up by the patterns or records formed.

"The force of the thought waves is spent in setting up the motion of these particles. These waves go out in all directions, but unless they strike a receiving brain they are lost in space. The particles are always in motion; they never stop except under spirit influence. The thought waves change their motion, and they come to rest after a length of time that is conditioned by the strength of the thought; the stronger the motion, the more pronounced is the record formed. When once at rest they form a permanent pattern. This might be compared to some of your physical laws. For instance, the blood remains fluid when confined to the veins and arteries, but when exposed to the influence of the air it coagulates. Do you see the comparison?

"We will have some difficulty in explaining where these patterns remain when once formed. The result of continued thoughts is not a series of separate patterns, but is somewhat continuous, like a ribbon. That description will have to answer, but it is not an accurate one at all. For in reality this roll of ribbon occupies no space at all. You can see here what difficulties we have in attempting to use material terms. But it will show you that there is thus plenty of room for unlimited records.

"Notwithstanding the fact that they occupy no space, they are yet visible, and are subject to laws of the controlling spirit, else they could not be recalled by memory. We see these patterns in your mind that are formed as you think, and we can see some of those you have placed away for further use. But we cannot see all of the latter, for, as we have said, the later ones more or less obscure those formed earlier.

"When certain patterns are made they sometimes have pronounced peculiarities, and if we continue to use material terms, we might refer to these as projections. These projections sometimes make contact with similar ones of other records that have been previously made.

256

This seems to connect them in a way that brings the second pattern into the consciousness—a process which we term remembering. When such an impression is recalled, the action of the mind causes other particles to adjust themselves to the pattern, making it slightly more prominent. This explains why, when a thought is recalled, it is easier to recall it a second or a third time.

"When one simply desires to recall a certain idea or pattern, his thought forms a new impression that makes contact with the old one and thus drags it to the fore.

"We use some of the impressions over many times, and by this use they finally become so prominent that they influence the action of the brain automatically, and in this way habits of thought are formed. And when such thought is associated with muscular action in any way, it results in habits of action and conduct.

"We would like you to think of this record as more or less continuous, but not exactly as a ribbon. The more exact picture would show it as discontinuous although not detached, if we can use that expression. We mean that it is discontinuous enough so that portions of it can be recalled without bringing all of it into consciousness."

'Now just what is this record composed of?'

"We have spoken of the moving particles. These are the foundations of life, the foundations of the universe. Your scientists try to conceive of something which they call ether. These particles are portions of that something. They differ from your electrons only slightly. But they are subject to separate laws, and are thus beyond the observations of your scientists.

"You have of course pictured these patterns as only a mortal mind can do. They seem like material ribbons. Here is where the physical and the spiritual world differ. When these particles adjust themselves into records, they are permanent. But permanency in the spirit world does not imply three-dimensional space. This we cannot make you understand. Spiritual laws are not the same as material laws, and mortal mind will have to content itself with our statements. To spirit mind these records are as solid as phonograph discs are to you. But, as we said, they occupy no space in a physical sense.

"Now if you have accepted our statements thus far, you are no doubt beginning to wonder what the will, the mind, is that controls this brain and these particles. I am afraid we will have to let you continue to wonder about that, for that is what we are still doing; and there seems no prospect of our solving the problem on this plane."

There was a break here for a week or more. Meantime Mary and Dee wrote the following in regard to what had already been given:—

"We will tell you about a trip we took to a far-away circle. We went to learn what we could about mind power. We knew the message was ready for you, and we wished to know more about the subject ourselves.

"We found a large circle who have made many investigations and experiments in the study of the action of one mind on another. They have invented many delicate instruments to record and measure the waves of thought. They record them in a way that resembles the phonograph. But these instruments are far more delicate and perfected than anything that earth people have yet contrived. We watched the work of recording our own thoughts. We could examine the records, and many times could recognize the thought, somewhat as we recognize a thought in your brain. You might call these records an artificial memory, for they are permanently recorded, and by experts can be read at any time. We could probably record our thoughts in that way for use in our libraries, although we have other methods that answer for the present. We think, however, that it may lead to a new way of recording for that purpose in addition to what we have.

"We were especially interested in the beauty of the patterns. You would not think perhaps that there was any especial relation between the beauty of the pattern and the beauty of the thought, but it is so, and markedly so. Perhaps this is a clue to the effect that beautiful thoughts have there on the appearance or features of the one who gives out such thoughts. It is a tremendous subject, and means so much in character forming. For if thought can form visible effects in material, how much more likely that it can affect the character, both of the thinker and of the receiver of the thought.

"We have seen no patterns that you could truthfully call pictures. They are representations of the special thought, and similar thoughts make similar records. But a thought or mental picture of a tree would not make a record that looked like a tree.

"At another time we visited another circle where they are experimenting with mind action, but they are studying it in a different way. They are watching the actual effects of thought on the brain itself. They are all very clairvoyant and can watch the disturbances set up by the thought waves. They have found that the results correspond to what has been learned in the other circle, so they feel that they are both correct in their conclusions. The teacher who is giving you the message has worked with these circles. He has made a long study of thought influence and can explain many things which we would not attempt."

Then, a little later, the first teacher made a summary of the statements first given and added a few comments.

"As Mary told you the other evening, we have invented many ways of measuring and recording the work of the mind. And a study of the records convinces us that we have arrived at the truth of a number of things.

"We find, for instance, that thought waves move in all directions and are lost in space unless they strike a brain that is in a condition to receive them. But the force of these waves does not decrease according to the distance. They are just as powerful after traveling thousands of miles as they are on the brain of one who is present.

"We have found that these waves are very much more penetrating than any material waves of which you have knowledge. No substance is dense enough to impede their progress. They can reach any brain no matter where the individual may be.

"We have told you that the spirit brain is composed of moving particles. You can imagine these particles moving in much the same manner as the electrons move in a material substance. But the laws which control them are entirely different. We believe them to be very similar to your electrons as to their origin, but just enough different to be controlled by spirit laws instead of material laws. We know that they are some form of force, and that they can combine in various ways. We do not know of any such combination, however, that is not caused by the action of the mind.

"When a thought causes a series of waves, these waves may reach some brains that do not respond. This is because the power of that brain is at that time being expended in some other way. But if it is in a passive condition they register by changing the motion of the brain particles from a circular to a wave motion. The motion that they ordinarily maintain is circular: not in regular orbits, but forming various spiral movements throughout the space which they occupy. Your electrons move about a nucleus, and thus are more fixed. We think that is the point that should be remembered in any comparison between the two.

"Now to sum up. The waves of particles are always subject to the power of the individual. We think, and the waves are formed by the thought. We make our brain passive, and thoughts from others can cause the particles to take up the wave motion. So long as their motion is circular they remain in motion. But the change to a wave motion brings them under the control of another law. When they

www.ingramcontent.com/pod-product-compliance
Lightning Source LLC
Chambersburg PA
CBHW032149080426
42735CB00008B/645